MW01038995

THE INVITATION

short stories of great encounter

SARA RUST

THE INVITATION

Copyright ©2016 by Sara Rust
All rights reserved

This book is protected by the copyright law of the United States of America. This book may not be copied or reprinted for commercial gain or profit. The use of short quotations or occasional page copying for personal or group study is permitted and encouraged. Permission will be granted upon request.

International Standard Book Number: 978-1480023093

To order more books or to learn more about the author, please visit the author's website:
www.saramrust.com

Printed in the United States of America

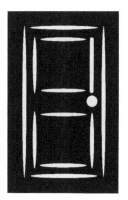

It's open.

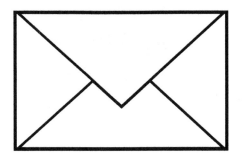

TABLE OF CONTENTS

1. TEA FOR TWO 1

2. DUST 9

3. THE STREAM 17

4. A RIVER JOURNEY 24

5. GLIDING 31

6. THREADS 38

7. ALTITUDE 44

8. NEW DEVELOPMENTS 53

9. THE DANCE CARD 62

10. THE STOREHOUSE 72

11. FLORA 82

12. PIE 89

13. SEASONAL 97

14. POTTED PLANTS 105

15. A FIELD OF DREAMS 114

16. LEGACY 128

17. FOR MY SCRIBE 138

Acknowledgments

To my Little Flock,

Forever and for always, thanks for the adventure.

Luke 12:32.

To my family,

For meals and a bed, and celebrating me always.

For being mine, and highly treasured.

And for responding in peace,

when trust and faith led me to a road less traveled.

To Lezlie, Cathy, Tami, Bernie, Kim, and Kate,

For friendship and prayers in my writing journey.

For critiques, and lessons, and encouragement.

For believing that gold was inside

and for helping me find and refine it.

PREFACE

I have always enjoyed a good story. I find I learn best and process most deeply through them.

I loved writing from a young age, but rarely took the time to do so after college. After many years of ideas brewing and buzzing within, I took the advice of one of my *heroes of the pen*, and began to write stories as gifts. It was just a way to practice writing and to bless some friends and family.

The Invitation is where I began. These were the first - a simple, but brave attempt to catch stories and insist they take root on a page. The journey of writing them was its own tale of wonder and intrigue, and love.

Like when Leea received *Tea for Two* for her Sweet Sixteenth, and then opened a gift from her grandmother that was a music box, just like Papa had given her in the story.

Or when I wrote *Legacy* for my grandfather, hoping to give it to him before he passed away. He read the story lying in a hospital bed, tears rolling down his cheeks. Over the next few days his health improved and he made a full recovery.

The Dance Card became a special eulogy for my grandmother when I read her story at her memorial service. Her story became a beloved tale to the residents of her retirement community – of hope, and redemption, and joy everlasting.

And so I continued to share the stories and read them aloud to small huddles of friends and family and classrooms full of children. All the while, Papa reminding me, *an invitation for one is an invitation for all.* The stories were written to a few, but the love they capture is all-inclusive.

I don't know what these pages may hold for you, but I can say that many have been loved by a great Love through them.

My great hope is that you will be too.

TEA FOR TWO

I MUST BE IN THE RIGHT PLACE, SHE THOUGHT. The invitation Desired One held in her hands had begun to glow. In front of her was a small stone cathedral nestled in the wood. Upon closer inspection, however, she discovered the building to be equal parts branch and vine and flower. She marveled at the architecture as trees wove with elegance around the stone walls. Above her hung a fragrant display of brightly colored flowers. Desired One brushed the stone work gently with her fingers and pressed her nose amongst the sweet flowering vines, drinking it all in. Holding the invitation to her heart, she sighed, *He's done it again*.

Opening the wooden door, she entered a little room. Her feet felt the earthen floor covered with soft green moss and purple clover. They were arranged, of course, with intent and design - a living, breathing mosaic. The sky was the only ceiling above the stone walls. Vines hung zigzagging from the surrounding trees, like green rafters. In the center of the room sat a simple, lovely table set for two, with a fine linen tablecloth and a tea set.

Desired One smiled at the sight of Him. He grinned as usual, delighting in His surprises for her. He felt sure He had outdone every previous one, as He always intended. Standing behind one of the chairs, He waited for her to approach.

"Please, come and have a seat." He motioned.

"It's very beautiful, Papa. What is this place?" Desired One walked towards Him and willingly sat in the chair He pulled out for her.

Taking a cloth napkin from the table, He waved it in the wind and laid it with care on her lap. "For today, I will call it *My Tea House*."

Desired One closed her eyes, shook her head a little and

3

smiled, while Papa took the seat opposite her. She looked back up at Him. His face was beaming, as if He couldn't believe His luck to be sitting down to tea with her.

"Papa, no matter how wonderful the surprise or how beautiful the setting, You always seem far more excited than I." She let out an easy laugh, "I'm not sure whose special day this is!"

He nodded with certainty and a smile.

"It is your special day, Desired One, rest assured." He leaned forward, "But I do take such joy in surprising you. I love to see you enjoy My goodness. A great pleasure, I admit." He winked and proceeded to offer her a scrumptious looking scone.

Desired One picked a raspberry-looking one from the tray and placed it on her plate while Papa poured each of them a cup of tea.

"One lump or two?" He asked, playfully.

Desired One picked up the cup, "One moment." She blew on it and then took a sip to decide how she would dress it up. After one sip, she giggled as she wiped her mouth, "None, Papa. It's perfect, as always."

"I know. Isn't it good?" He added.

"It's delicious. Didn't even burn my mouth. What kind of

tea is this?" she asked taking another sip and tasting the scone.

"I call it *The Wonders of New Adventures Tea*," He offered joyful-ly, knowing how she would like it.

"Of course! It could never be just plain spearmint, could it?"

He shook his head, "No, no. Not for today, not for your spe-cial day. I made it especially for you, for your new season, Desired One."

"Am I to expect new adventures, Papa?"

"Oh my, yes," His feet danced as he clapped His hands.

Desired One marveled at Papa's childlikeness.

"Yes! New adventures, my little one. Very precious ones. I can't wait to hear the stories you'll share this time next year." Again He began to clap his hands, which only made Desired One struggle to sip her tea between giggles.

"But first," He said putting His hand on her arm, "I have something for you."

This time Desired One put down her teacup and clapped her own hands. She loved presents from Papa. Papa bent to His side and picked up a beautifully wrapped box. It was small, covered with silky, iridescent fabrics gathered at the top and fastened with a ring of small white roses. Desired One's eyes widened.

"It's so beautiful, Papa, I don't even want to open it!"

"Oh, but you must." He said handing it to her.

Papa moved her dishes as she placed the present in front of her and began to slowly unwrap it. She playfully placed the ring of roses around her wrist like a bracelet and draped the fabrics across her shoulders like a regal wrap. Papa looked on with amusement. Upon unfolding the last fabric, she caught her first glimpse of a small music box. She looked questioningly up at Papa, wondering if there was something she was supposed to twist or pull.

"Just lift the lid." He nodded.

As Desired One opened the box, the music emerged with an almost tangible personality. It was as if an entire miniature orchestra was somehow hiding inside. She gazed down as angelic voices and instruments she didn't recognize rose majestically out of the little box.

"It's the sound of heaven?" She asked with awe.

"It's the sound of the Kingdom," He said, "in you." He smiled. "This is the sound I hear from my Kingdom in you. This is what I hear when I think of you, Desired One. I wanted you to hear how beautiful the song of your spirit is to Me - the music of your life and love for Me. There is no other like it." His eyes filled with tears.

And so did Desired One's, but before one could drop from her eye, Papa brushed it away.

"I've been collecting those," He offered, as a tear streamed down His own face.

She nodded, knowingly. Desired One loved the music box. It looked so simple on the outside, but was filled with such a wondrous sound. "I love it, Papa." She placed her hand on his and gave it a squeeze.

"It's funny, Papa," she said lost in admiration.

"What's that, Desired One?"

"It seems the more I come to You, wanting to love You more, the more I seem to discover how much You love me. Sometimes, I wish I had more to offer You." She looked at him apologetically.

"I love to love, little one. It is my greatest desire. I am satisfied already. I need nothing from you. When you enjoy being loved by Me, I feel your love."

With that, Papa stood up and extended His hand to her. "Would you like to dance, little one?"

Desired One rose, giving Papa her hand. With all the kindness and gentleness He had, He gathered her up into His big papa-bear arms, turned to the table and lifted the lid from the music box.

As the music rose seeming to live and grow, Papa and His Desired One twirled and spun on the cool mossy floor, under the green floral rafters, in the living stone cathedral hidden somewhere in His Kingdom.

DUST

Dust. *For miles and miles*, that's all he saw.

Trusted squinted to see if there was anything around him besides sand. He stood in the middle of what might have been a road, though he thought his surroundings too bleak to need one. He pulled the envelope from his back pocket and turned it over to see if he had overlooked some detail on the back. Nothing. Shrugging his shoulders, he tucked the invitation back into his pocket and looked up again at the sea of dust.

In the distance, he saw an odd shape breaking up the horizon.

It grew. Quickly. As Trusted's eyes focused, he noted that the object was accelerating towards him, kicking up dust. Soon he discerned the outline of a vehicle. It approached faster and faster until, in a thick cloud of dust, it came to an abrupt stop beside Trusted.

He waved his arms trying to see and coughed, clearing his lungs. The dry mud caked on the fenders, the smattering of side door scratches, and the dent on the rear bumper suggested the jeep had been on its share of journeys, despite its youthful canary color. The driver rolled down His tinted window.

"Are you ready, Trusted, or do you want to stand here all day?" Papa teased.

Trusted's face brightened as he nodded. He strode around the jeep and climbed in.

"You invited me to a desert?" Trusted asked playfully.

Papa grinned as he put the jeep into gear and pushed the gas pedal. "So it seems," Papa motioned for Trusted to fasten his seatbelt. "But I have it on good authority that sometimes the best adventures begin in the desert. I think you might agree soon."

Trusted laughed as he looked out the window at the great sand-scape. "Truthfully," he confessed, "it wouldn't matter if it was all sand, Papa. It's just good to be with You."

Papa elbowed Trusted. "I know," he agreed, "It's enough for me too."

Conversations were interesting with Papa. They didn't always require words, but their honesty and clarity was undeniable. As Trusted sat there, quietly appreciating this sacred time with Papa, something caught his eye outside the window. The sand that had so pervasively surrounded them began to morph. The more they drove, the more the ground beneath them turned shades of sapphire and cobalt. In a few blinks, the jeep was driving on a huge body of water. It rode smoothly, as if sliding on ice, though to Trusted's eyes the water appeared quite choppy.

"Want some tunes?" Papa asked as he checked his rear-view mirror. Trusted smiled as he looked out the back windows wondering if someone was actually going to pass them.

"Sure, what do you have?"

"Anything you want."

"I don't know, Papa. Surprise me."

Suddenly a song filled the vehicle. The music was alive with unfamiliar voices and instruments. It perfectly reflected the landscape outside. The notes and melodies were in sync with the water, and the clouds.

"That's quite a song, Papa." Trusted said with a whisper, not wanting to disturb the music around him.

It was then that Trusted could see a mountain range standing in the midst of the water. Cloaked in emerald and olive foliage and speckled with colorful flowering trees, it was breathtaking. The jeep slowed as they drew close, until Trusted could make out a road creeping up the side of the mountain range. Only in the Kingdom, Trusted thought, would there be a road around a mountain accessible only by water. As they neared the mountains, Papa switched gears, and they were on solid ground again, ascending the road around the scenic range. They passed large waterfalls and overlooks. The view of the water they had crossed was spectacular as the jeep continued to climb.

Papa turned to Trusted with a quick wink as they followed the road into a tunnel. Trusted could see the light at the end and was eagerly anticipating whatever was on the other side. Papa slowed as they approached the tunnel's end and drove out onto a huge overlook. The jeep came to a stop and Trusted examined the interior of the circular mountain range. It was like a great earthen coliseum. Waterfalls, flowers, and varying rocks adorned the sides of the mountains. All around the mountain walls were tunnels. Each one arranged with purpose, illuminating the coliseum with brilliant beams of light.

"Wow," Trusted whispered finally. "I've never imagined any place like this."

Papa closed his eyes for a moment, letting a thoughtful grin break across His face. "I'm so glad you like it."

"I'm so glad You thought to bring me here."

"There are some things I have for you, Trusted, for your special day." Papa got out of the jeep and walked to the back to open the rear door. Trusted followed suit.

"I have waited a long time to give these to you," Papa said patting a large duffel bag full of surprises. "I like to call these *the generation gifts*."

Trusted looked at Papa puzzled. "I'm not quite sure I understand, Papa."

"For generations your family has sought My face and asked for marvelous things from My Kingdom. Many thought these gifts would be for them, or their children, or their children's children. Some, in desperation, cried out for anyone, in any generation who might be ready to receive. None of them knew you, Trusted, but they hoped for you."

Trusted's eyes were glued to Papa's.

"I've never forgotten their prayers, Trusted. They were precious to Me." Papa's heart was stirred. With glee, Papa simply put His arms around Trusted and embraced him, "I am so excited to give these to you!"

Tears began to stream down Trusted's face as the significance of these gifts overwhelmed him. "I'm not worthy of this, Papa."

"It's not about being worthy, Trusted. It's about being ready." Papa patted his back and turned to open the bag. "You simply said *yes*, so I started filling the bag."

Trusted peered into the bag. Inside was a collection of ornately wrapped boxes and bags carefully placed so nothing would get bumped or broken. The gifts appeared aged, yet striking, an assortment of items from throughout the centuries. Papa reached behind the duffel bag and pulled out a hiking pack.

"Put your gifts into this pack as you open them. I want you to keep them close to you for whenever you need them."

Trusted reached into the bag and pulled out a simple package. He carefully peeled back the wrapping and opened the box. He pulled out a shiny gold key.

DUST

"Ah, yes. A very good gift, indeed, Trusted."

"What is it?" Trusted asked, turning it over to see if it were somehow inscribed.

"A key to the Kingdom."

Trusted nodded. "Which part?"

Papa smiled, "For Me to know and you to find out."

Trusted unwrapped the packages, piling the treasures in his pack. There were keys, fragrances, songs, open doors, joys. He looked at every item, not always sure their purpose or role, but understanding their great value. As he opened the last gift, Papa handed him a map.

"What is this?"

"A map to a part of the kingdom I would like for you to explore." Papa handed Trusted the keys to the jeep. "Your bag is packed for your journey. The sights and sounds are sure to thrill you. But keep in mind, Trusted, that this journey will not just be for you, but for the generations after you. You will release things to fill their bags and bless them on their journey." Papa closed the back of the car and gave Trusted a hug.

Trusted got into the driver's seat, and leaned out the window looking towards Papa.

"Enjoy the journey, my Trusted." Papa pointed back towards the tunnel. Trusted started the car, waved his hand, and heard again the living music flowing from the speakers.

"I always do," Trusted said as his heart filled with gratitude and expectation. Opening the map, he wondered at the possibilities. Taking a deep breath, he winked at Papa, put the jeep in gear, and headed out to use his great inheritance in the wilds of the Kingdom.

THE STREAM

T*HE RAIN WAS LETTING UP.* They each approached the dwelling place from opposite sides, entering through ornate wooden doors. Both wiped the rain from their brows and wrung their damp clothes. As they looked across the room, they caught each other's eyes. Smiling, they held their invitations to their hearts. Somehow, they understood He had been planning this all along. They had hoped He might invite them into His presence together.

The stonework and stained glass windows around them gave the impression of a chapel. Steadfast studied her surroundings. A peculiar sight caught her eye. Flowing through the middle of the room, a stream bubbled along as a refreshing song.

Peaceful approached the stream and knelt down. He cupped his hands to take a drink. Steadfast met him there. They beamed as they drank the delicious water, and then fondly asked to see each other's invitation.

"This is so fun," Steadfast remarked, "I've never heard of anyone being invited with a friend. Usually these invitations are for one-on-one adventures, aren't they?"

Peaceful nodded. "I think, perhaps, there is something special He means to show us together," Peaceful paused as he scanned the chapel. "Where is He? I didn't think He could be late."

As soon as Peaceful finished, they heard it. A playful melody rose from a grand piano by the large window at the front of the room.

I don't remember the piano being there, Steadfast shook her head. He always knows how to make an entrance, she thought. Steadfast and Peaceful stood to their feet and approached the piano. Papa sat behind the keys. He played the simple song with fervor. Steadfast and Peaceful grinned at each other.

"Good song, don't you think?" Papa finally asked as His

fingers continued to prance atop the keys. "It gets better. Wait for it," Papa grinned. He nodded over his shoulder directing their attention to the large window.

Through it they saw miles upon miles of the Kingdom. As Steadfast and Peaceful looked out, they heard voices join in with Papa's song. The melody streamed through their ears, as images formed before their eyes through the window, as if watching a movie. Faces. Then more faces appeared, until they saw a multitude of faces turning towards the face of God. They saw themselves preaching the Word to crowds of people, worshiping in various nations, and training up their own strategic family. They saw themselves writing books and embracing children, releasing secrets from His throne room and fishing for men. As they delighted in the visions, they gently reached for each other's hand, and Papa's song came to an end.

"It's time for a new assignment," Papa announced, "and bigger dreams." He turned and made His way to the unusual interior stream. Steadfast and Peaceful followed.

"New assignments?" Steadfast asked.

Papa nodded. "Yes. These plans are special. They require two to work as one."

19

Peaceful squeezed Steadfast's hand as they both looked at Papa with anticipation and a bit of trepidation. Papa sensed the mix of emotions.

"No, no, my doves," He comforted, fixing His eyes on theirs, "do not be anxious about anything. You are able, because I am able. And though it's true a great adventure lies before you, I assure you this journey is for your great pleasure." Papa winked, "And for Mine."

He bent down, motioning them to sit. Steadfast and Peaceful joined Him, sitting comfortably along the side of the little stream with their bare feet dangling in the water.

"I love this little stream," Papa shared, playfully kicking water on Peaceful and Steadfast until their faces shone with amusement. "It wasn't always here, you know?" Papa added.

"I don't understand, Papa," Steadfast ran her fingers through the water.

"Do you see how the stream starts over here, but also over there?" He pointed to two different springs coming from opposite sides of the room.

Peaceful and Steadfast surveyed the water flow. "I hadn't noticed that, actually," Peaceful admitted.

"Not long ago, the water sprang up from those two places. Isn't that interesting?" He kidded. He always knew the answers to His own questions, and was simply pointing out some delicious revelation when He asked them. Peaceful and Steadfast, of course, opted to play along. After all, it was fun to see Papa excited about these things.

"Where did the water come from, Papa?" Peaceful asked, leaning in towards Papa.

"What a fine question, my son. The answer is simple," Papa smiled, "The water came from you."

Peaceful and Steadfast looked at each other puzzled.

Papa dipped His hands in the water again, enjoying its simple pleasure. "It's love. And you two have been leaking it into this special place for quite some time."

"We've been leaking love?" Steadfast marveled cupping her hand to draw some water. Studying it, she contemplated the oddity that was her love manifest in a stream of moving water.

"Living water, Steadfast, not just moving." Papa offered, knowing her thoughts, as always. "This kind brings life."

"And the streams merged?" Peaceful pondered.

"Yes, you see, as your love for each other grew, the water

21

began to converge. Come, I must show you something." Papa rose motioning the two to follow Him down stream to the other side of the worship house where the water flowed out beneath the stone wall and beyond the great window. The stream expanded as it poured out of the charming chapel. What was only a stream in the worship house became a great river in the hills beyond. Past the hills there was a hint of a greater body of water. Papa, Steadfast, and Peaceful stared at the stream's flowing love amassing in the distance.

"Our stream did this?" Peaceful stood, mesmerized by the sight.

Papa nodded. "Your love for each other is beautiful to me. It is powerful in my Kingdom. Do you see how it waters the land? Never underestimate the power of loving another. This, my children, is really just the beginning."

Steadfast and Peaceful looked at each other in amazement, and again feasted their eyes on the sight beyond the window. "What manner of love is this?" they considered.

Papa looked at His precious children with much pride and joy. He loved love. He loved watching His children love *love* and lose themselves in its limitless wonder. "Are you ready?" Papa began.

Steadfast and Peaceful turned to each other and smiled,

holding each other's hands and looking to Papa with delight. "Let's begin then."

"We are gathered here today," Papa began, taking their hands into His, "to join Steadfast and Peaceful in a holy covenant..."

As Papa's words filled the air, Steadfast and Peaceful heard His song in their spirits, and around their feet they felt the increasing flow of their stream of great love.

THE RIVER JOURNEY

T*HE RIVER WAS CLEAR.* The sky was blue. The breeze was refreshing: a perfect day for a perfect surprise. Reward wore an inspired grin as she placed the woven-paper invitation into her pocket and stared at the meeting place.

"I knew it," she said, "I knew we'd meet here."

On the bank of the river, nestled beneath fragrant rose-draped trees, Papa sat quietly in a canoe. As Reward's eyes met His, a smile un-abashedly melted across His face.

"My Reward," He said with a sigh. "How do you like her?"

Reward approached the boat, feasting her eyes on its intricacy.

She'd never seen anything like it. Its sides were stunning, inlaid with swirls of wood and twirls of gold. The design was an impressive mixture of nature and royalty.

"I love it, Papa," Reward finally offered after drinking in every detail. "It's beautiful."

Papa nodded with ease. "What do you say we take her for a spin?" Papa held out an oar, also made of inlaid wood with gold flourishes. Reward clapped her hands, pranced towards the canoe and climbed in, taking hold of the oar.

"Are you ready?" Papa asked as Reward steadied herself. She gripped the oar with expectation.

"I'm ready." Together they back paddled, turned, and started down the river.

"I'll steer." Papa offered. As He called out directions from behind, Reward kept up. Occasionally she glanced down and caught the sight of the design on the oars coming alive. The gold inlay expanded and spread through the water like wings or fins.

Nearby trees gave off a sweet aroma as they swayed on the riverbanks. Flowers cascaded down their branches, painting them with tropical hues. Reward leaned back and forth and turned side-to-side trying to see the waterfalls she heard behind the branches. She caught glimpses of rolling green hills and mountains in the distance.

Gemstones sparkled beneath the clear water with colors Reward had never seen before. As they paddled around a bend, Reward saw a school of small dolphin-like creatures jumping, gliding, and spinning through the water. As Reward and Papa passed them, they gathered around the canoe. Half went gracefully under and around the boat. The others tumbled over the canoe like acrobats in the air. As they leapt, they treated the travelers to a refreshing shower.

"I love this," Papa sighed. "I love to show you these things. I love to hear you laugh, My Reward, and to laugh with you. I love this special time on your special day."

Reward turned back to see His smile, "Me too, Papa. Me especially."

"Reward, I have been steering the boat." He glanced down at the river pausing, "Would you like to steer the water?"

Reward looked at Him rather puzzled, "Um, what?"

"It's beautiful, isn't it? This water? And so full of life. Where would you like it to flow?"

"Papa, I'm not sure I know how," Reward looked down at her oar wondering how to use it to divert the water beneath her. As she toyed with it, she thought, *what do I do? Just think - River, flow left?* Before she could shake her head in disbelief, she saw the water beneath her shift its flow towards the left. She rubbed her eyes.

"That's my girl," Papa encouraged.

She thought right, and the river shifted to the right. Back and forth, the river shifted as Reward perceived its new path in her thoughts.

"Look ahead, my Reward." A little way ahead the river dropped off. Reward knew they were heading straight for a water-fall. "Where do you want to steer this river, Reward?"

Reward knew she was safe with Papa, but the physics of the situation challenged her.

Knowing exactly what was on her mind, Papa simply offered, "Why don't you try that?"

As the boat approached the falls, Reward looked up to the sky, and before she could close her eyes in anticipation, the water gathered beneath the canoe and lifted the travelers up. Papa and His Reward were soon floating on a river suspended in the sky, extending whichever direction Reward could put her mind towards.

As Reward looked back at the drop off, she saw the waterfall descending hundreds of feet to the pool far below. As Reward gained confidence in steering the water through the sky, she heard Papa's voice again.

"I think you might enjoy it, Reward," Papa mentioned, again knowing of the direction she was dreaming. "Just go for it!" Without hesitation, the canoe and the river began to soar through the sky, looping around, upside down, and dashing in between the clouds. Thrilling scarcely described the journey. The sound Reward loved the most, Papa laughing, roared behind her. Reward slowed the water and turned the canoe to get a good look at the new river in the sky. Rippling waters meandered in the open air, dripping on the land below. As the sun shone through the droplets, rainbows filled the atmosphere.

"Wow." Reward exclaimed.

"Do you see what's below us, Reward, where the water is dripping?" Papa pointed to the land.

Reward looked down and saw the outline of nations she knew well.

"We've been riding over the nations?" She asked.

Papa nodded. "You have steered the water well. See how it waters the nations? We are quenching their thirst with living water, my Reward!" He clapped his hands with joy, "This is so fun!"

"I don't feel like I've done much, Papa." Reward said still staring at the wondrous rainbows and river in the sky.

"This, my beloved, is what happens when you delight yourself in Me. Our adventures together change things. People. Nations. And you." Papa touched Reward's shoulder and nudged her to turn around to face Him. He took her oar and placed it inside the canoe. Face to face now, Papa lovingly took Reward's hands in His. "This is my good pleasure, Reward. To be here with you, to show you what we can do. I wanted to show you this river, and let you discover how it has no limits. No boundaries. There is no place it cannot flow, if you will allow your mind to dream. There are rainbows and showers of grace yet to pour out. He squeezed her hands and stroked her head with fatherly love. "Reward, this canoe is yours. I built it especially for you. Anytime you want it, it'll be here for you."

Reward was captivated by Papa's face. Such unequaled kindness, such thoughtfulness and tenderness always radiated from His smile. "Oh, Papa," She shrugged her shoulders as her eyes began to tear. "You are so good to me."

Papa leaned forward and kissed her forehead, "My great delight, dear one." He wrapped His arms around her and held His precious daughter close, "Where to, now, Reward?"

Reward leaned back from His embrace and smiled. She looked off to the side, dreaming up a course for their river of life. With a jubilant gasp, Reward scarcely had enough time to turn around before the canoe took off again, this time on a direct course for someplace below, a place hidden in the heart of a nation.

While the river continued to drip, and the rainbows continued to sprout, the sound of two great adventurers laughing filled the land as Reward and Papa steered the boat and the water through the dreams of her heart.

GLIDING

MUSIC FILLED THE AIR. Affection's spirit caught it like a sail in the wind. If she positioned herself one way she caught the rhythms of an African drum circle, another way and her spirit rested on the waves of a symphony. Everything about the atmosphere here was charged, whether with color or sound or emotion or wonder. Everything spoke life and creativity. It was the environment Affection was created for, and the one that was created for her, a perfect intersection of her purpose and destiny.

Arms open wide, she stood on a grassy overhang, absorbing the majesty of her vantage point. This land had no shortage of stunning landscapes. Down below and stretching for miles before her were strange, large mossy rock towers. She had never seen anything like them and wondered about their significance. She glanced at the invitation in her left hand. She loved the delicate vine décor that wrapped itself around the invitation and ended right at the place where Papa had lovingly written her name.

As she waited for Him, she couldn't help but dance to a Salsa melody her spirit picked up on. Little did Affection know, Papa had already arrived. He watched her as He stood beside some trees. He loved to watch his children's responses to His Kingdom. And in this case, He was captivated by Affection's dance of delight.

Watching intently and tapping his foot to the rhythm of her dance, Papa waited until the perfect moment to enter Affection's dance circle. With girlish glee, Affection squealed when Papa arrived on the scene seemingly out of nowhere, and led her through the most intricate and gravity-defying dance she'd ever attempted. With a final spin, Papa led her right back to where she started with arms stretched out gazing at the mossy pillars. Winded, Affection whispered, "What do you call that dance Papa?"

"I like to call that little number *The Dance of my Affection*," He winked.

Affection laughed, "It's a fun one, Papa." She bent down to catch her breath. Papa chuckled.

"Little lady, you ready? We've got a big day ahead of us." He slipped back behind the trees and returned to the grassy overlook with shiny fabric, rope of varying sizes and poles gathered under His arms. Within a few minutes, Papa constructed a splendid contraption.

"She flies like a dream," Papa said stroking the iridescent pearl-colored wings of the hang glider. "Shall we get strapped in?" Affection stared at the glider. It was stunning. The wings twinkled as she tilted her head left and right. She couldn't help but smile. Though a thought both fantastic and unnerving brewed in her mind, for Papa would surely be asking her to hurl herself off of the overhang momentarily.

Her feelings leapt off her face. He gently walked up to her and took her hands, "Affection, I will do the flying. I just want you to use your eyes." His head tilted as if desiring some confirmation that she understood.

She nodded and joined Him in the hang glider. Once they

were strapped in, both stood with their hands on the crossbeam looking through the wide-open air before them. She felt His sure hands on hers as she gripped the bar, and felt again the sweet assurance of all His Words. She knew His promises always rang true. His face broke into a grin, "Ready?"

On the count of three they launched off the overhang. Affection squealed with delight as the glider soared into the open air. Up and down, banking side to side, the glider flew with grace and freedom. "Affection!" Papa shouted through the sound of the rushing wind, "Open your eyes!"

Feeling the confidence of the air catching the wings above, Affection opened her eyes. She gasped, not out of fear or shock, but at the sight of what lay below her and Papa. A great river wove amongst the rocky towers below them. The waters swirled around the pillars, in some places like a calm stream, and in others like a raging rapid, with waterfalls sprinkled throughout. She rubbed her eyes at the waterfalls – for some behaved as one might expect while others surged with water flowing up, not down. She felt a tap on her hand. "Pay close attention, Affection. We're going to the headwaters."

The glider descended and gained speed. The river's great width began to shrink as Papa and Affection came closer to the source. Her eyes widened as she studied the landscape passing below. The rocky towers she had seen before, tall and moss-covered, were replaced by smaller rocky towers. Soon small, smooth towers replaced the rocky ones. And then the smooth towers were replaced by large, brilliant gems. Emeralds. Amethysts. Rubies. Diamonds. Opals. Sapphires. The water around them sparkled with color.

"I'm going to put us down over there." Papa pointed towards a little grassy field next to a small stream. Gently, he brought the glider down to a bank beside the headwater. Papa and Affection unstrapped themselves. Papa took Affection's hands and helped her up, then turned her around to see the horizon of great gems rising from the water. Affection's eyes watered at the sight.

"What is this, Papa?" Her eyes journeyed from left to right, mesmerized by the giant glistening jewels. He loved watching her undone by His wonders.

"These stones used to look like the ones you saw at the beginning of our flight, tall and rocky, covered in moss. Had I taken you further downstream you would have seen taller towers, whole hills, and after some time, we would have come to a mountain range."

Affection knelt on the water bank, unsure of what any of this meant. After taking a moment, she looked up at Papa who stood beside her. "Papa, what is the meaning of this – why are you show-ing me this?"

Papa knelt down beside Affection. "Because you, dear Af-fection, put the stones in the water. You flung the mountains into the great river. Your great faith in Me has been telling mountains here and there to jump into the sea. You declared something over here. You believed Me for something there. And as you have been busy displacing rocks, I have been busy letting My water flow." He scooped His hands down into the water. "My water. My Spirit." Papa let the water drip from His fingers then scooped up more. So enchanted by the water, Affection waited for Him. "It's very agile and strong, don't you think, Affection?"

She nodded.

"I love to see it work. It has taken the mountains you placed in it, and discovered the jewels within. Some mountains were always intended to be jewels, you see. A royal diadem for my Kingdom." Papa took His hand from the water and faced Affection, placing His hand on hers. "This has brought me great joy, Affection, this work of your life. I desire to show you how you have done these things. You must be attentive to my voice, do you understand, Affection? For I have not only shown you these things to bless you, to reveal to you that you are one who takes the mountains, but I desire to train you to show others how to do the same. To teach. To train. To mobilize." Papa looked back out into the great body of water, "There are more jewels to be found, my Affection, and you will need help."

Affection felt His peace. She was ready for His lessons.

"How about we get a closer look at one of these things?" He winked.

Affection smiled and nodded. Papa took her hand and walked her over to a little boat resting on the bank, already full of climbing gear and a picnic basket. Papa helped her into the boat, and the two set sail through the water towards the nearest sapphire with ropes and carabiners in tow.

The cadence of their conversation filled the air as the two explorers talked about life, the Kingdom, and the great quest for hidden treasure yet to come.

THREADS

WINSOME AND FIERCE, THE WIND SPUN AROUND HER. She felt its strength and its care as it blew by, playfully whipping her hair. Standing atop a grassy plateau she looked below at the ocean. Her eyes looked far to the horizon then rested, watching the rhythmic waves crash against the cliff wall below.

Emerald sighed, "I think I could stay here forever." She clutched her invitation to her chest.

"You can," quipped a familiar voice, "but I have more to show you today." Emerald turned to see Papa.

"Papa!" she squealed as she ran to Him. He ran towards her so fast that she barely took two steps before He scooped her up and held her, her feet dangling off the ground in a sweet embrace.

"My Emerald, so precious to me," He whispered in her ear. "What a privilege to be here with you."

"You mean for me to be here with You, Papa. It's my privilege, of course!" She said as He gently placed her on the ground.

"Oh my little Emerald, I have it on good authority that your delight for Me could never surpass My delight for you; but you go right ahead and try, my child." Papa winked.

"What are we doing today, Papa?" Emerald asked as she held her invitation up and grinned.

"My children always want to know all the details. Do you grow tired of my surprises?" Papa kidded.

Emerald lovingly batted him with the invitation.

"I've been planning these things since before time began. It's honestly one of my favorite hobbies," said Papa with a smile as He turned. "Come along then, Emerald, we're going for a little walk." Papa walked away from the cliff edge down through a pasture to a fragrant, flower-sprinkled woodland at the other side of the field. Emerald followed along after Him. Papa walked with purpose straight towards a drape of greenery at the edge of the wood.

"It looks pretty dark in there, Papa."

Papa took her hand in His, and with His other peeled back the curtain of vines. He smiled with certainty, and led her into the darkness.

Emerald's tentative steps were met with an extraordinary sight, for as she moved into the dark wood, the flowers all around her began to glow. They started gently at first, but soon the light from the petals had created a promenade of color, illuminating a well-worn path that darted back and forth through the trees. Papa tenderly drew her hand to His chest and stopped. He looked around the festive display and sighed, as if He was seeing it for the first time. This was quite untrue, however, for He Himself had worn that path practically smooth as He traversed His Kingdom.

Papa carefully led Emerald step by step down through the trail, drawing her attention here and there to the flowers. He would lift them to her face inviting her to smell their fanciful perfume. Strangely, each flower emitted a different quality of the Kingdom. *How could this be?* she wondered. One smelled of peace, another joy. Or expectation. Or hope. Or family. Or friendship. Or faith. Or love. Or humor. Or home.

"Papa, how do you dream up such things?" Emerald breathed. She looked up at Him, pulling herself away from the flower she was smelling.

His eyes fixed on her, "It's easy. I think of you, and the rest just comes."

At that moment, from a branch above her head, a new flower blossomed. Its colors were unlike any of the others Emerald had seen in the wood and its fragrance could only be described as *affection*.

"See?" Papa said, nodding at the flower. They grinned at each other and the marvel of this place. "Come, Emerald, there is more," Papa prompted as He took her hand again and picked up the pace. The flowers grew dim as Emerald saw light begin to break through the distant trees. She thought they must be getting to the other side of the wood.

Papa drew back the leaves at the edge of the wood and led Emerald out to a grassy ledge of a large canyon. The crevasse was so deep she could not perceive its end. The canyon walls extended far to the left and right in splendor.

Stretched across the wide expanse were cables of color, like large, long strings of yarn. Their colors were familiar now as she recognized them in the flowers she had seen in the wood. The cords were gathered in various places across the canyon and intertwined in elaborate patterns, forming large woven bridges. From the sky, Emerald imagined it looked like giant scarves had been strung across the gorge as far as the eye could see.

"It's beautiful, Papa, but," she tried to understand what she was seeing, "what are they?"

"Some call them mantles, others blessings," Papa smiled. "They are mantles of motherhood."

Emerald blinked, confused.

"Strands of faith, love, family, strands of friendship, hope, and affection - each woven together in their own unique way. The flowers you saw are used for the dye, you see? And then the strings are woven into a blessing, a calling, an anointing, a preparing. You have been busy, Emerald."

She shook her head, "I've been busy? I don't understand, Papa."

"Your life has woven a great many blessings, Emerald, a multiplication of profound proportion. You have allowed My Word and My Kingdom to come into your heart, and as you have loved Me, and loved on the ones I have brought to you, you have been weaving. You have woven these blessings - and they are beautiful."

Papa's voice trembled recalling the beauty of Emerald's life laid out for Him so that His own family would expand. He reached down for her hand.

"Would you like to release some today?"

Emerald gazed at the mantles just below, astonished with the thought that her life had created something so immense - an architectural feat of the Spirit. She had not realized what she had been building through her quiet, hidden life and simple devotion to Papa.

"Yes, Papa, let's release them."

Papa took her hand and placed it on the edge of the mantle below them and with one touch, the mantle blew up from both sides of the gorge and gracefully began to descend into the beyond. "For the Kingdom, Papa," she proclaimed looking up at Him, "and for our family."

Papa nodded. "For the Kingdom, and for our family, Emerald." He led her along the edge of the canyon to the next mantle. With a loving touch, Emerald's blessings of a mother's love began to fall, one by one, to clothe the next generation.

ALTITUDE

I*T COULD HAVE BEEN MORNING*, if morning existed in this place. Everything was crisp and new. The light shone throughout with a gentleness and expectancy. The air itself was completely refreshing and even slightly sweet.

From her back pocket she pulled out her invitation. The colors on the page were rich. Hues of crimson, earth, and moss flowed in glittery arches and swirls. Within the design, His calligraphy invited her to this very place.

Wonder stood atop a high, rocky spire. Its flat landing was

not very large, but allowed enough room for a meadow covered with tall, soft grass and an occasional wildflower. She wasn't sure how she'd gotten here, really. All she could remember was hiking up a mountain trail into this small meadow. Turning around she noted the trail was now gone. Wonder quickly removed her shoes and walked around the landing. Her feet felt warmth from the kind grass while her arms danced in the wind. She looked down the sides of the spire seeing nothing but sheer cliff walls and distant clouds below. Discovering the great altitude at which she stood, she stepped back from the edge.

"Pretty good view, Wonder?" came a voice from behind her. Wonder turned to face Papa and nodded. She drew near him for a much anticipated and desired embrace.

"It's good to be here, Papa," Wonder sighed.

"Yes it is," Papa said, "This is always a good place to be." He gently released her from the hug and held her hands. "Are you ready?" He asked.

Wonder shrugged her shoulders and smiled, "I think so, Papa."

He nodded. "Good. This is going to be fun."

And with that, He let go of her hands, turned, and ran off the edge of the spire. Wonder blinked a few times trying to comprehend what had just happened. There was no doubting Papa had just flung himself over the cliff's edge.

She peered over to see his small body still free falling towards the clouds below. Suddenly she could hear His familiar, though distant, voice.

"It's best if you get a running start, my Wonder!"

Wonder grinned with the realization she was about to participate in one of her greatest dreams. "We're going to fly," she whispered. Without hesitation she ventured to the other end of the landing to get a running start. Barefoot and arms pumping, she sprinted across the small meadow and with one last step vaulted into the open air. This might prove to be her fondest playground.

Down, down, down she fell. As the wind swept around her, she was encompassed by joy and began to twirl. "Papa!" She yelled trying to figure out where He had gone.

At once she saw Him zoom upwards past her, flying back towards the landing. She looked up and tried to see what He was doing. Then he fell again until He was free-falling right beside her.

"Hold out your hand, Wonder!" He instructed. With all her might she reached out her hands to either side of her and felt the powerful grip of her Papa on her right hand. She felt herself slowing down, until she had stopped moving altogether.

Papa grabbed both her hands now, until her head was right side up again and the two stared at each other with great amusement.

"I'm floating!" Wonder exclaimed.

"Yes, you are, my Wonder. Fun, isn't it?" Papa released her hands. "I'm fond of floating."

Wonder looked down, "This is incredible, Papa."

Wonder laughed uproariously while spinning somersaults in the air. Papa, always up for a good laugh, eagerly joined her.

When the two high flyers finally regained some composure, Wonder remarked, "How am I doing this?"

"One touch from my hand, Wonder, and reality is altered. I was reminding you what you were made for. One touch of my hand, and your body begins to remember. Of course, one must be willing to jump before one can fly. But I felt sure you were willing."

"I knew it. I knew I was born for this."

Papa laughed. "And for so much more."

Wonder's eyes widened as she stared at Papa.

He laughed again. "How about we play a game, my Wonder?"

"Done." She was in total agreement. *Flying games with Papa, how could you pass that up?*

"Okay, good. I'm glad you are so agreeable," He joked. "Here's how you play. We have five minutes to fly to the lowest place we can, and bring back to this place something we find. Best discovery wins."

Wonder nodded. She knew she was at a slight disadvantage and the probability of her actually winning this game was slim. But in her spirit she knew His games seemed to never be about winning, but discovering. "This should be fun," she thought.

Papa began, "Ready? One...Two...Three!"

Before Wonder could turn herself around to begin her descent, Papa was gone. Wonder swooped through clouds, swishing and somersaulting, as she tumbled her way down. She passed through the last layer of cloud and saw the land below. Slowing her descent, partly to plan her strategy of finding low ground, she admired the scenery - so foreign, yet so familiar.

Wonder took a deep breath. *Home*, she thought, looking at the Kingdom. *All the goodness of Papa's heart transcribed in landscape.*

Studying the land she noted the mountains, hills, lakes and seaside. *Surely something by the sea*, she concluded. *That would be as low as flyers go.* Wonder made her way to the beach. Drawing close to the ocean's edge, she saw a pod of massive whales soaring across the water.

Floating now, she was caught by the sight of these large creatures flying through the ocean. Wonder's eyes widened. She glanced over to the beach, and back to the whales. With a smile and a dream, she shot straight up into the air. "How low can I go, Papa?" she questioned aloud. And with a fiery sense of adventure, she peered down to determine where the lowest seabed might be. With a keen eye, she calculated her approach and headed into the ocean.

"Let's see what this body was made for!" She yelled with anticipation.

She gained incredible speed then dove into the water and headed directly beneath the whales and the waves. It didn't take Wonder long to realize she could breathe underwater, and that flying in water was much different from flying in the air. She was surprised, though, that the water didn't seem as difficult to move through as she had supposed, and even though she plunged deeper and deeper, she could see everything with clarity.

Then she saw it, as if it were placed there for the purpose of this little game. At the bottom of the seabed sat a small golden box inlaid with stones. The box sparkled in the light. Wonder carefully picked it up and opened it. Inside rested a simple gold necklace. The chain was thin and unassuming. At the end hung a gold disc engraved with something, though Wonder couldn't make it out. With no time to lose, Wonder put on the necklace, closed the box and returned it to the ocean floor. With a wish and a way, she darted straight back up into the sky.

Moments later she was high above the Kingdom just below the clouds, and in a few more moments she neared the meeting point by the rocky spire, where Papa was floating quite patiently. She came to a gentle stop right beside Him. Spotting the necklace around her neck, He smiled. "You are good at this game," He encouraged.

"The whales helped, Papa," Wonder admitted, slightly out of breath.

Papa smiled knowingly, "I thought they would."

"It's a neat little necklace, Papa, but I..." before she could finish, Papa took the necklace from around her neck, held it in front of her, and began to blow on the little gold disc which in turn began to spin. As she stared at the spinning disc, the engraving became clear, and animated. It was a pair of wings waving up and down. Papa winked, touched the disc to stop its spin, and began to blow it in the opposite direction. Wonder smiled as she now saw a pair of fins waving up and down.

"The only difference is altitude," Wonder mused.

"There are no limits here, Wonder, just uncharted territory. You are my sign and Wonder, child, for you are willing to go beyond the confines of logic." Papa placed the necklace around Wonder's neck, and lovingly kissed her forehead. "You are my favorite, my Wonder, and surely you will teach others how to fly."

Papa reached into his pocket and pulled out a small pearl. He held it out to Wonder in the palm of His hand. "This is a dream for your life, my child. A flight school. For I desire many who will fly high and see the landscape, and many who would fly low and discover the hidden treasures. Through you I will bring great multiplication. Time will give testimony to my faithfulness."

Wonder slowly reached out to touch the pearl. "Papa, where did you find this?"

"I went low, to the deepest place I know - your heart, my Wonder." Papa smiled and embraced her, "I always find good things there."

Wonder rested in His arms, "You win, Papa, you win." She felt His gentle laugh.

"No, no, my Wonder. We win. We always win." He squeezed her with tenderness and joy and the two began to spin upwards. Papa took Wonder by the hand and the aerial ballet continued.

Somewhere high above the clouds and the rocky spire, Papa and His Wonder danced and darted with agility and grace beyond logic and imagination, enjoying each other's presence and the release of fulfilled dreams hidden in the depths of His children's hearts.

NEW DEVELOPMENTS

H ARMONY DECIDED IT MIGHT BE BEST to walk in a circle. Perhaps a change in perspective would clue her in. The invitation wasn't exactly straightforward. It didn't surprise Harmony, that instead of a precise location, she would find a riddle tucked inside. She knew Papa was quite fond of them.

For if you are to find the place of invitation

Do not look past the imitation,

For your eyes will desire, to see a great spire

But all you will see is the breeze.

Tread forth, make haste

For He lovingly waits

Where the bees love to buzz

And the owls perch above

And great beauty is found

By the one who is willing

To see what is blowing in the wind.

She stood in a simple green field. Flowers poked up here and there, biding their time in the breeze. On the outskirts of the field were trees whose branches twirled along the ground. As Harmony walked in circles around the field, she looked intently for anything that might tie into Papa's riddle. Where were the bees or the owls? Where was the spire? *So strange*, Harmony concluded. It was a place marked with purpose, but little else.

"Look carefully." Harmony heard a familiar voice whisper from behind her, "Try not to be distracted by what you perceive, for truly there is no lack here."

Harmony turned to look at Papa. But there was no one behind her. She heard Him again, "I'm inside. Look carefully."

Harmony looked around the field again. "Inside what, Papa?" She asked.

Suddenly, Harmony felt a breeze begin to blow on her back, then around her neck, and up upon her head. It was a peculiar breeze, to be sure, for it did not flow in a stream, as she was accustomed. Instead, she felt it weaving around her, embracing her as it continued its hidden choreography.

With the arrival of the breeze, she noticed an odd addition to the scene. Was it a fabric? It was hard to tell. It moved like fabric, sheer and shimmering, suspended in the air. She could see right through it, but when the wind blew, she could tell it was there – like someone had put a giant sheet atop a large building. It reminded her of the walls of the ancient tabernacle that were comprised of thick cloth. Grateful to the breeze, she now saw a door into the fabric edifice.

Inside, the view wasn't entirely different, for she could still see the field and the trees and the sky above through the fabric. But now she could see Him.

"Blessed child." Papa remarked as He immediately approached Harmony and embraced her. "So good of you to come."

Harmony smiled, "This is some place, Papa."

Papa nodded and held out his hand inviting her to follow Him further into the building. "It is a very special place to me, my Harmony. I can't invite everyone here. Sometimes it's hard to wait for the wind to speak. But for those who are willing, it doesn't disappoint."

Harmony took His hand and followed Him through a hallway. A breeze proceeded their steps, allowing the fabric to catch the light and shine just enough for Harmony to make out its edges. Harmony and Papa walked to the very end of the hallway where an entrance marked the way to a large room. The supernatural tapestry that encased the space expanded high into the sky, like the spire of a castle, and Harmony knew instinctively she could smell the sweet aroma of honey. As she looked down at her feet, she noticed the grass that had been beneath her was no longer. Instead her toes tapped upon a mosaic of inlaid wood. The walls of fabric, though still transparent in areas, would at times appear solid and decorated with gold vines and flowers.

"Here we are," Papa exclaimed, "this is where we shall play today."

"What shall we play, Papa?"

"One of your favorite games, of course." Papa spread His arms out and spun around the room, "And what an amazing space to play it!"

Harmony seeped through memories and thoughts to remember which favorite game this room seemed so perfect for. Papa stood delightfully with his hands on His hips watching her think. Then a thought jumped from years past to the forefront of her mind, "We're going to build something!"

Papa nodded with a grin. "I believe you used to begin by making the roads for your little towns on the floor. But roads will not be our first step." Harmony looked at the room, the wooden floor, and the billowing walls. It was perfect for building a small city, but she wondered what they might use to build it.

"What is the first step, Papa?"

"There is no use in putting down roads, or raising up buildings, in planting trees or releasing the animals. First, we must establish the atmosphere."

"The atmosphere," Harmony spoke softly to herself.

Papa drew close to Harmony, "Life can not exist without the proper atmosphere. And Harmony," He took her hands into His, "you are very accomplished at creating atmospheres for Kingdom expansion." Harmony felt the intensity of His words at her very core.

"Let's begin."

With Harmony's hands in Papa's, He winked, and then led

her in a dance around the floor. Filled with joy from head to toe, Harmony giggled. Papa twirled her around and around until finally they stopped in the middle of the room.

"And that's how we release love and joy," Papa declared. Harmony looked around at a room that was teeming with love and with joy. She could almost see it with her eyes. "I thought perhaps we would declare things like, *let there be light*."

"We can, my love. Declare away. It's only that sometimes the things we say don't require words."

Harmony understood. And without delay she began to skip around the room singing songs from deep within. She would stop to raise her arms and brush the air only to begin spinning again. And from the middle of the room she could hear Papa's rhythmic voice as He began to speak forth all that she was declaring, "There's hope. Peace. There's conviction and passion. Adoration! Authority. Faith and rest. Expectation. Healing and maturity." The atmosphere was filling up.

Harmony had become so lost in her dance of creation, that she didn't notice all that was happening in the room. As she turned around to face Papa again, she saw the once wooden floor covered with a rich miniature landscape. She saw mountains and rivers, waterfalls and forest beautifully laid out across the floor. Harmony carefully made her way back to Papa trying cautiously not to step on a tree or a mountaintop.

Papa covered His mouth sheepishly, "I'm sorry my Harmony. You did such a great job on the atmosphere, I couldn't help but start creating."

Harmony smiled and hugged Papa, "It's okay Papa, I like when we work together."

Papa smiled knowingly, "As do I."

He took her hand and they crouched down together to look at the landscape. As Harmony looked at a large forest on the left, Papa's eyes were on a mountain range to the right. From both directions a flock of owls emerged and flew swiftly towards one another. As their eyes followed the birds, they saw the flocks converge and realized that the other had been busy creating the same little flock at the same time.

"Great minds think alike." Papa mused.

Soon the little land beneath them was teeming with life. Harmony could make out small villages emerging by bodies of water. As she thought of the roads necessary to connect them, they simply began to appear. And as if watching some amazing time lapse of history, she saw the villages begin to grow into small towns and then small cities.

The sight was astonishing. And she was lost in it again.

"This is one of my favorite games, too, Harmony. Most especially when we get to play together. Now remember, my child," He stretched out His arm across the room, "what you loose in heaven, will be loosed on earth. When we play, it is powerful."

Harmony took a deep breath and nodded, "I believe it."

Papa turned to Harmony, taking great joy in looking at His child. "You make me so proud, little one. Harmony, your life is bringing restoration to a creation that had been brought to ruins. It was always my hope that my children would take pride in the family business. But not all do. In you I have found one trustworthy of great inheritance. Please forgive me," Papa winked, "If I pour it out on you in abundance. But I have found you ready to receive."
He grabbed Harmony's hand and looked back at the small world growing beneath their feet. "You *are* ready to receive," He confirmed gently.

Harmony felt a deep love welling up inside her. Standing next to Papa, looking at their co-creation filled her with the greatest sense of life. She was thankful.

Papa and Harmony watched the room fill with life and light and hope. A tear rolled down Harmony's cheek as Papa smiled, both knowing that somewhere in the shadow lands their little game was becoming reality.

THE DANCE CARD

S*HE COULDN'T HELP BUT DANCE.* Reaching her arms to the
left and right, Fearless twirled with her head thrown back
and eyes marveling at the great height of the ceiling. The walls
extended so high above, it was hard to see the rafters. The
room was circular, large enough to move with a bit of expres-
sion and freedom, but small enough to feel intimate. Rows of
large arched windows, trimmed with delicate gold leaf, lined
the white walls. She felt the smooth floor, flat as a rail, beneath
her feet. Marveling at its serene blue color, the floor reminded

her of a still, calm lake. It looked so much like water. Fearless kept reaching down to inspect the floor, making sure it was dry.

Incredible, she thought looking around the bright, airy room, *and impeccably clean.*

In her hands, Fearless held her beloved invitation. It was hand crafted, a decoupage with dried petals of all her favorite flowers. The invitation was folded in two and had a gold ribbon attached to the top so she could tie it around her wrist, she supposed. She thought that was a nice touch, as she would never want to lose such an invitation. She took a deep breath. Waiting for Papa was always filled with excitement.

She heard him coming from outside. The sound of His voice was unmistakable, but today it was downright intoxicating, for Papa was singing:

> *Come, My Fount of every blessing,*
> *Tune your heart to sing of grace*
> *Streams of mercy, never ceasing,*
> *Call for songs of loudest praise.*

By the time Papa had made His way around the little building and entered the door, He was whistling. Approaching Fearless, hands behind his back, he continued to whistle while His eyes smiled. He took in the sight of the beautiful room with His lovely child waiting with her invitation now wrapped around her wrist. Stopping before her, He winked, and brought His whistling tune to an impressive finale. Fearless grinned. Papa followed suit, opening His arms to embrace her. "Welcome, my child."

Speechless, and resting in His arms, Fearless simply nodded. Finding her hands, Papa twirled her out from him until they stood hand in hand admiring the room again.

"How do you like it, Fearless – my dance hall?"

She gazed around the room again. Biting her lower lip, she turned towards Papa, a little reluctant to tell Him what she was thinking.

"It's okay, you can say it." Papa assured her, nodding.

"Well – it just seems a tad small. Even for just a pair of dancers."

Papa drew his hand up to his chin and placed a finger on his lips as He considered her words. He looked up squinting, trying to make out the rafters high above. Shrugging his shoulders, he looked down again at the floor beneath their feet. The corners of his mouth began to curl up as he looked back at Fearless, "I suppose it depends on how you dance." Clearly not concerned with the dimensions of the room, He clapped His hands together, changing the subject. "Now, first things first. May I see your dance card?" He pointed to the invitation hanging from her wrist.

Fearless looked down, *so it was a dance card*, she thought. She passed it to Papa who opened it like a detective on the prowl for clues. He began to shake his head. Fearless had read the invitation at least a half a dozen times and couldn't imagine what He was reading that would illicit such a response.

"This simply won't do." He said finally.

Fearless folded her arms. "I'm not sure I understand, Papa."

He pointed to the dance card, "Why, your dance card is already full!"

"Full?" Fearless hadn't seen a list of dance partners on the invitation.

Papa nodded. "Would you like to see?"

Fearless timidly reached out her hand and opened her dance card again. She now saw a list inside the invitation. Sure enough her dance card was full. But where she expected to find a long list of old friends and beloveds, she did not. She knew these unexpected partners, however. She was acquainted with Worry and Anxiety, with Sadness and Hopelessness, and the others that had found their way onto her dance card. But she had no desire to dance with them, and grew increasingly upset over the simple fact that there was no room left for Papa's name.

Papa approached tenderly. "Are you ready?" He pulled something out of His pocket and handed it to Fearless. Looking down she saw in his palm a small pink eraser. "I think you've danced with them long enough, Fearless, don't you?"

Fearless looked down at her list with understanding. They were not the dance partners she had desired to find on her list, but she knew the truth of how often they had come to ask for a turn around the floor throughout her life. Their steps were careless, repetitious, and unforgiving. She didn't remember exactly when she'd ever agreed to dance with them, but glancing down at the eraser, she knew it was time for them to go.

Papa closed His eyes, a smile breaking across His face as Fearless took the eraser from His hand, placed the dance card in her palm and went to work. With the removal of each name, Fearless felt a sense of increasing freedom within. Finally, her dance card was empty.

Fearless took a deep breath. She turned the card towards

66

Papa. "Empty." She offered.

Papa took the dance card in His hands, took a gold fountain pen from his pocket and signed His name. He turned the card towards Fearless. "Full." He confirmed. There on her dance card written in gold ink, large enough to take up the entire list, was Papa's name. He grinned as He placed the card around her wrist, "I'm afraid this pen doesn't erase."

Fearless laughed with relief, "That works for me, Papa."

With that settled, taking each other's hands they journeyed to the middle of the petite dance floor and stood waiting. Waiting was always purposeful in the Kingdom, Fearless reminded herself, though often her excitement was hard to keep at bay. Nodding His head to an inaudible beat, Papa began to whistle again. With gusto, He began to spin Fearless around and around the dance floor. Soon, the little tune Papa whistled with fervor filled the hall from floor to ceiling. The sound became fuller as they danced, and though Fearless couldn't figure out where the rest of the music was coming from, she had her suspicions the walls had chimed in.

The room was filling with energy and great joy. Papa was apt on the dance floor, twirling and spinning Fearless. His fingers bounced to the music upon her hands. Time and time again His head flung back in sheer delight. Fearless laughed as she watched Papa, but felt assured this room was too small to contain the dancing Papa was working up to. Not to mention it was getting rather warm on the dance floor.

Curiously, Fearless suddenly felt something on her feet. It was cold. It was wet. It was refreshing. It was most certainly - water. She broke her gaze with Papa to glance down only to see the solid, serene blue floor beginning to lap upon her feet, and crash gently against the walls.

"Here it comes!" Papa said, pointing to His ear directing Fearless to listen to the music. The music began to swell, and with it the water below their feet. With a crescendo, Papa and Fearless shot up into the air atop a wave of water. Papa smirked as the water lifted them high and began to descend again. "See, plenty of room to dance," Papa explained, looking at the still greater expanse above.

The water below mimicked the music surrounding the happy pair, and they danced amongst the waves as the water lifted them up and down and spun them around in the dance hall. At one point, the water carried them halfway up the room only to even out at that level and become solid and sure again. Papa slowed their pace to allow them a breather, until they had stopped altogether, standing on the curious blue floor hundreds of feet above where they had begun.

"So courageous, Fearless." Papa held her face in His hands. "So brave. You were created for this – to dance in freedom and joy amongst the waves of life." He took a step back and grabbed her hand. "This is what I see when I think of you, my Fearless. A great dancer, who has learned how to take my hand, and simply dance to the tunes I whistle. There is no other like you."

Fearless smiled bashfully. "Papa, I haven't always felt so courageous," she admitted.

"Sometimes, Fearless, courage is subtle. Sometimes it's a quiet prayer, a simple knowing, a simple trusting that I am who I say I am, and deciding to dance with me when there are no clear answers. I think you are far braver than you know." Papa placed His hands on her shoulders and drew her close. "I want you to believe what I say about you, Fearless. Whether you see it or not, whether it feels true or not, simply believe."

Fearless considered His words. His countenance held such assurance. Of course, Papa was trustworthy. Of course His words were true. Why was it so hard sometimes to believe the good things He had to say about her?

"Fearless," Papa said knowingly, " sometimes we get used to

dancing with other dance partners. We hear the things they speak to us and begin to believe it as truth. I assure you it is not. And I assure you as you listen to my voice while we dance, you will soon forget what they had to say."

Fearless closed her eyes. What a beautiful thought, to forget all the lies the others had spoken. What a wonderful reality, to believe what is true. With her eyes closed she began to raise her arms. A dance was forming within her heart, and she let it flow through her limbs. Papa watched with excitement – the dance of truth, He thought. Fearless began to dance around the blue floor, and soon Papa found His step right beside her. She could hear the familiar song bubbling up from within Him:

Come, My Fount of every blessing,

Tune my heart to sing of grace

Streams of mercy, never ceasing,

Call for songs of loudest praise.

Fearless continued, "Praise the mount! I'm fixed upon it, mount of Thy redeeming love."

As the music swelled and the water began to shift again, Fearless caught the sight of the windows in the dance hall beginning to open. Soon, the water began spilling out of the windows as it rose and dipped in the dance hall. Peering at the scene again, it became clear that Fearless and Papa were dancing in the midst of a great fountain. The dance hall itself had become a great fountain. Fearless and Papa splashed atop the water as it careened up and down following their musical lead.

This was the fount of blessing, Fearless understood, this place of dancing with Papa, splashing about in joy and freedom. And to her great delight she knew, the dance had only just begun.

THE STOREHOUSE

IRONIC THAT THE INVITATION SHOULD LEAD ME HERE, He thought. Courage stood on a dusty country road between two fields of tall cornstalks. The fields extended as far as he could see along the sides of the road. At first, the site was a little disheartening. He hoped upon receiving such an invitation that he would see something extraordinary. But here was a simple cornfield. A sight that was as familiar to him as his right hand. He walked up the road, kicked the dust, looked around and waited.

"Rather ordinary, isn't it Courage?"

Courage turned to find Papa standing with one messenger bag slung around his shoulder and another in his hand. His eyes spoke of peace, his slight smile hinted of adventure. The Divine encroached on the ordinary, and all of Courage's interest was piqued for what the day might hold. *If He can turn water into wine,* Courage mused to himself, *I wonder what He'll do with this ordinary field.*

Papa nodded knowingly, aware of Courage's thoughts. "Guess we shall see." Papa grinned. Approaching Courage with arms open, Papa embraced this son, "Glad you could come."

Courage sank himself in Papa's arms as if he were five years old again. "Good to be here," Courage whispered as he tried to hold back tears.

Papa hugged Courage tighter for just a moment more then handed him the extra bag, "You'll be needing this."

Taking it, Courage deftly wrapped the bag over his shoulder and examined it.

"We need to collect some seed," Papa said. He nodded towards the dry corn stalks, ready for harvest, and invited Courage to join him. They walked down the road by the field, plucking ears of corn here and there. Not far along the road, Courage heard a sound behind him. The landscape was somewhat arid, but he was sure it was the sound of running water. He looked over his shoulder to locate its source. Papa kept plucking corn, smiling as usual.

Sure enough, trailing behind him and Papa was a small stream. It needed no ditch to follow. It faithfully made its own way heaped up on the ground. Water emerged and joined the stream from the very places where Papa and Courage had plucked the corn. Even more curious was the way the stream stopped just behind Courage, like an obedient, playful puppy. Courage grinned, turning around to face the stream. Looking up at the next cornstalk and back down at the stream's edge, he took a step backwards. The stream followed him, stopping just before bathing his feet. Courage reached out and plucked an ear of corn from the stalk beside him, and without hesitation, clear, crisp water began to flow out from the bottom of the stalk he had just harvested.

"Funny thing, that water," Papa stared amusingly at the precocious stream, "Somehow, it can't help but follow the seed."

Papa held up his finger to tell the stream to stay. He winked at Courage and turned to continue their journey. Courage followed. Papa snapped his fingers by His side and the water continued to follow them from behind.

Papa and Courage continued until they came to the top of a

hill. From the top, Courage could see a plot of land that had been tilled and readied for seed. Papa motioned Courage onward until the two of them were beside the tilled field. The stream, following close behind, obediently stopped beside them.

"Now we plant the seed," Papa instructed.

Courage, feeling confident about planting the corn, began to gather kernels from inside his satchel. After pulling out a sufficient handful to scatter, he hesitated at Papa's outstretched arm bidding him to wait. Courage watched intrigued and mused, *perhaps there was a different strategy for sowing seed here.*

Papa crouched down, looking across the field like an expert golfer sizing up his final putt.

"What are you doing, Papa?" Courage asked.

"Deciding." He whispered, suggesting to Courage the delicacy of the moment.

Courage bent down next to Papa and whispered back, "Deciding what, Papa?"

"Everything." Papa scanned the field before them. He picked up some dirt in his hand and rolled it through His fingers.

"You mean, where to plant and all that, Papa?" Courage offered timidly.

Papa's eyes fixed on the field as if even now He was planning it all out. "Before I decide where, Courage, I must decide why. Everything begins with a purpose."

Papa brought out a handful of kernels from his bag, only now the seeds were not simply corn kernels. Papa's words interrupted his thoughts, "Unique. Each one. No two are ever the same. That's part of the challenge, part of the fun." He grinned. "There is a purpose for which I will plant these seeds. I will let them grow in freedom, though I will tend to them, that their purpose will be fulfilled. And you, Courage, will help me plant."

Courage's eyes widened. Instinctively he reached into his bag and pulled out a handful of his own unique seeds.

"I know what we are building, now." Papa confirmed, "Let's plant."

"Don't you mean, growing, now? You know what we are growing?" Courage questioned.

Papa simply remarked, "You'll see." He began to walk out into the field dropping seeds here and there. He made it look haphazard, though Courage knew there was a purpose behind how and where every seed was planted. With Papa, there was always purpose. Papa turned towards him, "Aren't you going to help me?"

Courage, who had been patiently awaiting instructions, shrugged his shoulders and lifted his hands, "Papa I haven't a clue where you want me to put this seed."

Papa nodded, making His way back towards Courage. "Do you trust me?"

Courage looked down at the seed in his hand and around at the field. "Of course," he sighed, "Of course I trust You, Papa."

Papa sighed too, and smiled with confidence, "Then just start planting seed."

Seed by seed, Courage began to sow the field. Sometimes he planted purposefully, taking one seed and placing it intentionally into a little patch of dirt. Other times he too would toss a seed here or there. He had no plans. He just tried to do what Papa did. Occasionally he obeyed Papa's instruction to put a specific seed here or there, but mainly he dropped his seeds simply in faith.

When all of the seeds had been planted, Papa and Courage walked back to the road where the stream had remained. Papa whistled a pleasant melody that sent the little stream into full motion, covering the field, and watering the seed.

As soon as the water had soaked into the earth, Papa began to blow on the field. Almost instantly, to Courage's surprise, little green shoots sprang up. They continued to grow up and out. Leaves sprouted and vines bloomed and crept upwards towards the sky. Courage noticed some of the vines, branches, leaves, and blossoms, beginning to intertwine, forming what Courage could only describe as an arch.

Surely, he thought, *that looks like a doorway.* He looked up to the left and right, *and those could be windows.*

"Is it a building?" Courage wondered.

Now, Papa moved towards the growing mass and began to pull and prune as He skipped about the field. He molded it as it grew. Courage stepped back as the building expanded higher and wider until Papa stood in the midst of the doorway and yelled, "Ho!"

With that, everything stopped.

There it stood - a grand entrance. The walls on either side of the doorway held little windows, with patches of flowers nestled underneath them creating the illusion of quaint window boxes. Moments before the field had been full of small wispy green sprouts, but now the plants had grown strong and thick, twisting and turning, fashioning a living front to a striking building. It was like a small manor house built solely out of materials found in a botanical garden. Papa stood enamored in front of it.

Catching his breath, Courage confirmed, "It's a building."

Papa nodded. "Actually, it's the beginning of a building." He walked over to Courage, "a special variety of building, in fact." Papa paused, engaging Courage's eyes, "This is a storehouse, Courage."

Courage nodded, trying to understand.

"Interesting little things, these storehouses," Papa explained. "Great doors and immense walls, but they never seem to end. Watch this," Papa motioned to his bag, "Plant another seed, Courage."

With that, Courage removed a kernel from his bag and placed it into the ground. Suddenly the seed sprouted and grew, joining the green framework already in progress. Courage saw how the walls of the edifice began to extend further out.

Papa's eyes twinkled as he watched Courage gaze at the movement and growth. He knew Courage was trying to make sense of it all, and was pleased at last to give him the insight he desired. "This is your storehouse, Courage. It has no end." Papa extended his arms to direct Courage's eyes around the storehouse. "You have been faithful to plant seeds, to invest in my Kingdom, Courage. And the seeds that you plant are not only building my Kingdom, but they are extending your storehouse. You have not always known what I was up to, but you trusted Me, and I have used it all. I had a purpose for it all, from the beginning."

Courage stared at his storehouse – intricate and beautiful. On his knees now, the reality of it all sunk in. The seeds were so small, he thought. And yet look at what Papa did with them.

"The storehouse is filling up." Papa spoke as he walked towards Courage. "You are laying up a great inheritance here, with your faith and through your love and service."

A question arose within Courage, "What seeds were you planting, Papa?"

Papa smiled, "While you were sowing time, talents, faithfulness, finances, service, and my Word, I was sowing my children. I was sowing you, Courage. Just as your seeds faithfully sown build a storehouse for your inheritance, my seeds faithfully sown build a storehouse for my Son's inheritance. I planted you, to reap a harvest for Him. You are His, and your inheritance is His, just as His inheritance is yours. It all works perfectly, really."

Papa joined Courage on his knees as they both looked at the marvel of gardening before them. Papa sighed, taking it all in. He then pulled out from behind himself another two bags full of seeds.

"How about another round?"

Courage smiled, and reached for one of the bags. "I'd be honored."

The field before them began to teem with life again as Papa and Courage spun and stomped and danced around planting seeds here and there, while the storehouse grew and the Kingdom expanded to the great amusement of the two giddy gardeners.

FLORA

THE ONLY LIGHT IN THE ROOM came from the window to her left. It ran the whole length of the room and extended from floor to ceiling. Halfway up the window she saw a balancing bar. Buoyant carpet covered the floor, and the walls were simple, tidy, and an unassuming gray.

The space was poised for movement, but consumed with stillness. Outside the window stood a majestic huddle of mountains, hills, and valleys stood.

Pure One took out the invitation from her pocket. She

double checked the time and location and traced her name affectionately with her finger. It was so beautiful. The handwriting was like no other. Even in the way He wrote her name, there was a knowing and delight.

"It's a prayer room." Papa said, startling her. She turned to see His sweet face as He moved forward to embrace her. "Thank you for coming."

Pure One nodded, always speechless at His gratitude.

"A prayer room?" she glanced around a bit puzzled, "What's with the balance bar, Papa?"

Papa pulled a familiar item out from the bag slung over His shoulder. "Do you remember these?"

Pure One looked down at a pair of small black ballet slippers worn by tiny feet many years ago.

"Yes." Pure One reached out to hold the precious shoes her grandmother used to pirouette and plié and spin in. "I gave them to my sister."

Papa smiled, wiping away a small tear, "That was very thoughtful." He looked around the room drinking in the sacred space. "You didn't know about this room when you gave those to her. Your sister had been coming here for years, actually. This is her prayer room. You see, when she prays on earth, she dances in heaven. It's rather lovely to me." Papa lifted the slippers to his lips and kissed them softly. He tenderly placed them inside his bag, " I wanted you to see this place first, before we go."

"Go?" Pure One asked.

"Yes, I have a very special place to take you today. But first I wanted to say, thank you for this room."

Pure One looked at Papa with some confusion. "I'm sorry Papa, I thought you said this room was for my sister. I don't quite see what I had to do with it."

Papa moved forward, placing His hands on Pure One's shoulders and kissed her on the forehead. Smiling with a comforting chuckle he remarked, "Ah. But you have very much to do with it. In fact, you built it."

Pure One looked at Him with great confusion, "I don't understand, Papa, I don't remember. I mean, how could I?"

Papa took her hand, and led her to the big glass window. As she looked out, she saw more than just the huddled mountains. Images of familiar things: places, faces, and scenes of her own life displayed as if on a screen. "I remember the years of separation. When you would cry out for your family so many miles away. Sometimes all you had was a sigh or a tear that I would take care of them and of you. I remember. I was there. And I answered, not just on the earth below, but here in the Kingdom. The Kingdom is more real than what you see. When you cried out for your family, I began to build this for your sister. It was time to prepare a place for her. In fact, Pure One, you have been part of building many things for many people. If you could only see the great work of what you call weak prayers." Papa chuckled again.

Papa turned to Pure One who was still mesmerized looking at the screen of moments in her life so seemingly small and insignificant, yet so dear.

"The prayers of the righteous accomplish much, and my Word, which I have deposited in You, Pure One, will never return void. You have helped prepare a place for her, now she goes to prepare a place for others. Both of you are building for your entire family," Papa looked deep into Pure One's eyes, "and I am very jealous for your family."

Pure One nodded, feeling within a great strengthening of faith. "Nothing is impossible with you, Papa."

He smiled and sighed. "We have lingered here long enough, are you ready?"

Pure One gathered her hands together, "Yes! Where are we going?" Papa shook His head and winked his eye, "Why, oh, why would I ruin the surprise?"

And with the blink of an eye, Pure One was sitting on a rock on the gentle slope of a hill, surrounded by mountains. A blanket of soft grass and a variety of rich, colorful flowers covered the slope. The aroma seemed was strong enough to lift you off the ground, twirl you around and place you back on your feet. It was an exquisite garden; a marriage of delicate detail and wild frivolity. Pure One looked around trying to take it all in.

"And this is what we've been building for you." Papa spoke softly not wanting to disturb the moment. "I'm quite fond of it."

Pure One walked through the flowers, occasionally bending to smell them. "It's breathtaking," she finally said, looking up at Papa with tears in her eyes.

He came alongside her and gathered her up in His fatherly arms. Pure One could feel the sweet rhythmic beat of Papa's heart.

"Come sit with me." Papa said as He took Pure One's hand and led her to a swing. The swing was handcrafted, by Papa, of course, and was made of sections of inlaid wood placed to look like a quilt. Golden swirls, rosewood, and cedar played about within the precious swing. Papa and Pure One sat together. She laid her head on Papa's shoulder as He gently began to swing them.

"I have something for you, Pure One." Papa said reaching into His pocket. He pulled out a small gingham pouch, tied with a satin ribbon.

"What is this, Papa?"

"Open it."

Pure One carefully untied the ribbon and unfolded the little pouch to find seven simple seeds.

Papa grinned, rather proud of Himself for thinking of such a gift.

Pure One smiled with amusement at Papa, "Seeds?"

"Yes! New seeds. New dreams. You see, my precious daughter, dreams are the flora of heaven, the garden of the King-dom. And I have some new ones to plant in your heart."

"What kind of dreams, Papa?" Pure One said carefully touching each one.

"I never quite know until they are planted. Funny, don't you think?" He said, giving her a tender squeeze.

"How do I care for them?" she looked up at Him earnestly.

Papa reached His finger over to touch the seeds in her hand,

"Drench them in faith, my child. Let your imagination shine bright on them, and allow the winds of impossibility to do their trick. No eye has seen, no ear has heard the things I have planted in your heart. A season of great dreaming is upon you, Pure One." He placed His hand now on top of the seeds and looked down at her, "I wonder how big we can get these new ones to grow."

Pure One smiled, feeling equally excited and hopeful.

The dreaming garden filled with the sweet cadence of Papa and Pure One's voices as they began to share the dreams of their hearts. The hours passed without bother as Papa swung and Pure One sat enjoying the sweet fragrance of the garden. And throughout the Kingdom the sound of gentle giggles could be heard as Papa and Pure One laughed at impossibility.

PIE

THE COBBLE STONE PATH INVITED HER FORWARD. It had none of the tendencies of normal stone paths - uneven and awkward when walked upon. The stones were soft, yet sturdy. Their dappled color ran through the woods like a ribbon. Faithful expected nothing less, of course. But somehow this place, though one expected it to be good, exceeded one's definition of good. It's true then, what they say, that the reality of the Kingdom lies just beyond the confines of the imagination, and stretches joyfully further and further than logic could explain.

Faithful meandered down the path taking in the peaceful scenery and enchanting scents of the woods. She pulled out an invitation from her pocket.

So odd, she thought, *it's smudged*. Upon closer inspection, she noticed little dried globs of - *jelly, maybe?*

Rounding the bend she saw an opening in the wood to a small field speckled with wild flowers. Beside the path sat a charming little cottage, complete with a stone chimney puffing away. This is it, she concluded as she approached the door. Inside she heard a sing-songy voice chirping away. The voice stirred a joy deep within her. The joy bubbled up from her belly and trickled out in soft laughter Faithful tried to keep inside. This is it, alright, she affirmed. Before she could knock, the door swung open with enthusiasm, and there stood Papa, his face alight, his chef hat slightly askew. His apron appeared to have seen its share of action that day and his cheeks were dusted with flour.

"Faithful!" He said with excitement. Her feet dangled above the floor as Papa gathered her lovingly into His arms and welcomed her in to the adorable kitchen. "Faithful! I'm so glad you're here!" When He finally put her down, she stepped back to get a good look at Papa. She wasn't sure if it were possible for Papa to be tipsy, but it would certainly be fair to say He was exceedingly joyful - and loud. "Faithful! Are you ready to have some fun?"

Faithful nodded and bit her lip trying to contain her excitement. He drew near her and energetically whispered in her ear, "We're making pie!"

For a few moments they held each other's gaze, but each could see in the face of the other the inevitable quickly approaching. Their eyes blinked, their smiles twitched, and even their eyebrows tried to cling to some kind of composure, but the joy brewing within both of them was merciless. At last, in unison, they burst into laughter, tears streaming down their eyes. Papa grabbed the counter to hold Himself up while Faithful conceded defeat and rolled about the floor chuckling all the while. Between breaths Papa and Faithful recounted, "We're making pie!" It only restarted the waves of laughter.

When the waves subsided, Papa and Faithful stood by a marble island in the middle of the kitchen, sipping on some water.

"Papa, you are too much. This kitchen is down right intoxicating!"

"Ah, yes. Joy is my favorite ingredient. I never cook or create without it." He smiled. He pulled out two oven mitts from a drawer and opened the oven door. A delicious fragrance wafted by her nose. Papa pulled out a pie, its filling bubbling up between the lattice crust.

"Wow, Papa, that looks amazing!"

"I'm sure it is," He said with a wink. "I can't wait for you to taste it." Papa blew gently on the pie and began to dish up two slices. Handing Faithful a fork, they playfully clinked their utensils together and dug in. Papa took a bite, and paused just long enough to watch Faithful take her first taste. Her eyes closed instinctively and her whole body, from head to toe, from flesh to spirit, was overcome with the flavor of the pie. She swallowed and peered up at Papa.

"What kind of pie is this?" She stared at it and back at Papa marveling at this holy concoction of fruit and buttery crust.

He happily stared back, amused by her enjoyment. "Fruit."

"What *kind* of fruit is this, Papa? I've never tasted it before."

"I was hoping you'd ask." He gently took the plate and fork out of her hands, and led her to the back door of the cottage. Upon opening the door, Faithful saw scores of fields and orchards ripe with fruit, none of which she recognized. She looked at Papa, desiring understanding.

"So much fruit, eh, Faithful?"

She nodded. "I've never seen these kinds of fruits before. Do you have strawberries over there? I can't quite make it out at this distance."

Papa shook His head. "No, no strawberries." He grinned. "No fruit like that around here."

"What kind of fruit is this, Papa?" She bent down to inspect the berry bush just in front of her.

Papa took a deep breath, "Well, a little bit of it all, really." He bent down next to her and pulled off some berries. He began to pop some in his mouth while He offered a few to her. She took one from His hand and carefully placed it into her mouth. Papa rose and began to walk between the rows of fruit.

"What does it taste like, Faithful?" He asked grabbing a piece of fruit here and there and licking His fingers in between bites. Strangely, as she began to taste the fruit she had only one word to describe its flavor, "Patient? It tastes patient. How can something taste patient, Papa? That's not possible."

Papa walked down a row of fruit trees, as Faithful jogged to catch up, "Interestingly enough, Faithful, you have just proven that it is possible." He handed her a round mauve fruit, "Try this one."

Faithful looked down and drew the soft fruit to her mouth.

93

She shook her head incredulously, and looked at Papa, "Goodness?"

Papa nodded His head, "Goodness. One of my favorites."

Papa and Faithful continued walking through the orchards and fields and vineyards. She marveled at the tastes of the unique fruit around her. Peace. Loving-Kindness. Salvation. Discipleship. Miracles - all wondrously delicious fruit.

Papa stooped to pick up two empty baskets beside an orchard. He handed one to Faithful. "We'll need some fruit for our own pie. Take your pick."

Faithful began to look around and pick out the most interesting fruit she could find to fill her basket. Papa stood back and watched.

"This farmland is amazing, Papa. It must have taken quite a while for all of this to be ready. There's so much!"

Papa nodded. "How long have you been fully alive, Faithful? How long have you truly known I was who I said I was?"

"Oh. A little while, I suppose, Papa."

He smiled, "We'll, it's taken about that long."

Faithful paused, with questioning eyes.

"This is your garden, my Faithful - your orchard, your fields, your vineyard. This is what your life in Me is producing, and even now, it's expanding."

Faithful looked down at her basket of fruit, and then around at all the bushes and trees and heavy-laden vines.

"My life? This is the fruit of my life?"

"Yes."

"But there's so much! There's so much, Papa, and it tastes so good."

"Yes there is, and yes, it does! Isn't it wonderful? The Holy Spirit cultivates wonders in a willing heart. Your life, Faithful, has transformed the landscape of the Kingdom, and there is still more to come." Papa walked towards Faithful and offered to carry her basket. Faithful complied with a smile. "I wanted you to understand the impact of your life, Faithful. Your thoughts and actions towards Me are precious. The seeds you plant, even when you feel they are insignificantly small, bear such glory, such beauty, such fruit. Taste and see, dear child, that the Lord is good."

Faithful lost herself in His gaze. He was filled with love for her. He was proud of her.

"And now," said Papa, "How about I teach you how to make some pie?"

Faithful nodded and wrapped her arms around Papa's waist.

He tucked her in close with one arm and held the basket of fruit on His hip with the other. They meandered back to the cottage with no thought for time. Soon two familiar laughs could be heard filling the cottage again as the smoke rose through the chimney within. The fruit simmered on the stove, all primed for this special day of making pie.

SEASONAL

A S SHE STOOD BEFORE THE GARDEN TOOL SHED, Harvest heard the lilting cadence of a fiddle in the distance. It was a beautiful garden, albeit small. The beds were meticulously kept. Not a weed in sight, just pristine rows of perfectly ripened fruit and vegetables. Rose bushes surrounded the small garden in a hedge with their blossoming aroma. Harvest reached inside her invitation and pulled out some fresh rose petals. Her nose took a deep drink of their fragrance. Then she leaned over to smell the roses on the bushes. *This is it,* she thought.

Seeing a chair on the modest patio by the shed, Harvest made her way to rest in it, all the while hearing the fiddle reels coming closer. Soon she heard the fiddle just behind her. Turning around she saw a jovial Papa, donning a straw hat, offering her His hand. "Let's show them how it's done, my Harvest!" Papa grinned.

Harvest smiled, and then curiously looked around for Papa's fiddle. His hands were empty. "You won't find it, dear one," Papa affirmed, "The music is stirring from inside you."

"But it got louder the closer You were."

Papa nodded, "Think of it this way; my Presence is a sounding board for the inner workings of your heart. The closer you get, the louder it resounds." With that, He reached out His hand. Harvest willingly accepted it and in a whirl, she and Papa transformed the patio into a wee Irish dance floor. Fiddle reels and laughs filled the small garden until suddenly the music stopped.

Harvest put her hands on her heart, "Oh no! I'm so sorry, Papa, the music is gone! I'm not sure what I did."

"No, no, my Harvest. It seems the song has only come to an end, to make way for a new song. Rest assured, the music only gets better from here. Now we can eagerly await the melodies to come."

Harvest let out a sigh of relief and both the weary dancers took a seat on the patio.

"What do you think of my little garden here, Harvest?"

"It's beautiful, Papa, though honestly I expected any garden of Yours to be a bit larger."

Papa smiled knowingly at Harvest, then turned to look over his garden, "This is one of the smaller varieties. I thought it would be a fitting place to begin, before I show you one of the larger ones." Papa stood up and walked to the tool shed. "We will need some tools to work in the other garden," he said opening up the door. "Pick one."

"Pick one?" Harvest rose from her chair and peered into the shed. Her eyes widened. Inside was an intriguing collection of typical garden tools and some not so typical ones. On the floor she spotted ballet slippers, on the shelf she noted a can of paint brushes and hanging on the wall was a simple fishing pole.

"But you can only pick one." Papa repeated.

Harvest entered the shed looking over the range of tools. *What should I pick? Was this a test? How could ballet slippers prove productive for a gardening task?* Scouring the shelves, the walls, and the floor, she finally came across an object that, though seemingly unfit for a day in the garden, was the only perfect item to be found in her mind. She carefully pulled it out from behind the shovels and hoes and dragged it outside to Papa, whose eyes confirmed His delight in her choice.

"Now that, dear Harvest, is a perfect gardening tool." He took the tall silver sword and rested it over His shoulder. "Follow me, Harvest."

Harvest and Papa proceeded through the small garden to a narrow dirt path on the other side of the rose hedge and began to follow it to where Papa only knew. Onward they traversed on the dirt trail, passing gardens on the left and right. Some were overflowing with vibrant flowers, some brimming with luscious fruit, and some were bursting with the savory smells of herbs growing within. Papa kept trucking along with His straw hat and sword. Harvest merely tried to keep up as her eyes wandered to and fro taking in the scenery.

At last, Papa's pace slowed. Harvest walked up beside Him to see the view. They stood on an unassuming green hill. Before them stretched a garden whose end, she supposed, was miles away, hidden in the horizon. The sight was unique to say the least, for even though the garden appeared manicured, tall fruit trees and flowering bushes sprouted up whimsically amidst the lines of strawberries and rows of cabbage. Harvest looked up at Papa.

He knew precisely what she was thinking and answered without missing a beat, "What?" He joked, "Sometimes as I pick green beans, I must partake of a delicious orange. I just like stuff where I like stuff."

She laughed, shaking her head.

Dropping the sword down to the ground, Papa whispered. The anticipation of the moment preceded His words, "Watch closely."

Harvest was not sure what she was looking for, but hoped desperately that she would not miss it. Her eyes were drawn to a large oak tree standing ridiculously tall in the middle of a pumpkin patch. Squinting, she did notice something interesting. Its leaves were changing color. Slowly at first...then quickly. In minutes, the leaves had fallen off the tree and new buds were sprouting. The new leaves grew large and green, only to begin to dry out and turn orange and yellow. Harvest was amazed. She saw the oak tree experience all four seasons in mere minutes. However, the pumpkins below seemed comfortably settled in autumn the entire time. As she turned to face Papa to inquire about this sight, she saw Him with the sword pointed towards the oak tree.

"Keep watching," He whispered again as he began to move the point of the sword towards other trees, bushes, and vines. As He waved the sword the seasons would change around specific plants or groupings of plants. He was conducting a seasonal orchestra. "Now," He handed the sword to Harvest, "it's your turn."

Harvest tentatively took the sword in both hands and looked around the garden. As she looked at the abundance of plants, something strange began to happen. There was a sense inside her, an undeniable feeling, that the apple tree beside the blueberry bushes was craving winter.

Drawing her sword with both hands, Harvest pointed at the tree, and at once winter came to the apple tree. It was soon followed by spring. She felt undeniably sure that the field of daisies were hungry for summer. Pointing her sword again, she saw the daisies perk up. With bewildered joy, Harvest began to wield the sword over the whole garden as the plants ebbed and flowed with the seasons. With her arms growing weary at last, she put the sword down.

"In this garden, Harvest, the seasons don't just happen, you see? Something inside the plants craves them. They hunger for winter and thirst for spring. The seasons enable the plants to grow, and I have placed destiny in their roots, that they may have an insatiable appetite to be fully matured." He looked down at Harvest and lovingly patted her hands on the sword. "You are a season shifter, my Harvest. You were created to shift things for my Kingdom. Shifting seasons - it's not about arbitrary change; it's about ushering in maturity. As you wield my Word, you will usher in maturity for my Bride. Your life, your declarations, your presence will bring forth new seasons for others to mature in. You see, in the Kingdom, seasons are like paint brushes, creating strokes of refinement, color, and vision."

Harvest just stared at Him pondering of all the implications of her life being one that initiated change and maturity in others. "But what if I bring about the winter season?"

"In the Kingdom it is not that winter means bad times and summer means good. The seasons aren't intrinsically good or bad; they are divine transitions that lead to maturity - especially if one's eyes are on Me. This is the transformational power of Truth, when it is wielded in season." Papa winked.

Harvest drew the sword near her to consider what Papa had said. Suddenly she heard the rhythmic beating of drums.

"A new song has awoken, My Harvest, from your heart."

Papa wrapped His arms around her.

"It sounds like an army."

He thrust the sword into the nearby grass, then took both her hands in His. Their feet caught the rhythm of the drums as they danced in a circle, both dreaming of a day when the bride would be fully awake, fully mature, and fully on the move.

POTTED PLANTS

COOL BREEZES DREW THE PERFUMES from the courtyard towards her. Incomparable beauty surrounded Chosen. Flowerbeds painted the courtyard with bursts of color and a short stone fence hemmed it in on three sides. On the other stood a small stone cottage. It reminded her of pictures she'd seen of Italian homesteads, complete with arched walkways and hanging flower baskets. In the center, a tranquil fountain bubbled happily as it passed the time. Smiling, she took out her invitation.

Carefully opening it again, she saw the beautiful sketch inside. It was not only an exact replica of the courtyard, but also a perfect rendition of it from the very spot from which she stood. "Incredible," she marveled. Hearing footsteps behind her, she turned and saw Him. Papa approached, arms laden with small potted flowers.

"Oh Papa, do you need help with those?" Chosen reached out to help lighten His load.

"My load is light," He said grinning as He placed the pots down on a nearby patio table, "but thanks for the offer." Brushing off the soil from His arms, He drew near to Chosen and hugged her. "Thank you for coming."

Chosen cleared her throat, unable to respond, overwhelmed with thanksgiving. He drew back to look at her. His eyes looked straight at hers without wavering. He smiled, assuring her she was in the right place, that He loved her, and it was okay to be so near Him. At once she felt the peace and ease of simply being with family.

Papa motioned to the potted plants, "Would you like to help me plant these?"

"Oh, yes! I would love to, Papa!" she nodded, as excitement grew within her.

He laughed at her zeal, "I was hoping you'd say that." He handed her a few pots and winked, "I could certainly use the help."

Chosen looked around the courtyard, wondering where there would be room to plant more flowers with the beds so full.

Papa watched her with amusement, "Where do you think we should plant them?"

Papa's voice brought her attention back to the flowers in the pots. Each was a brilliant color. The petals and leaves varied from long and feathery to thick and waxy. The more she investigated one plant, the more amazed she became by its color, or texture, or smell. She tried to decide, where the best place to plant them would be. "Honestly Papa, I don't see a lot of room here in this courtyard. These flowers are so exquisite, it seems like they should be planted some place where they can be seen, and not lost in the crowd here."

Papa drew in a deep breath and nodded. "Where might that be, Chosen?"

She peered around again at her surroundings. Papa obviously knew far better than she the answer to that question, but Chosen felt honored He wanted her input.

"Well, I think only a place of beauty would befit such flowers."

Pleased that she gave her opinion, Papa nodded, "Go on."

Chosen's eyes drifted up towards the sky as she tried to think of good places. "I'm thinking - beside a waterfall or atop a mountain or maybe in a quiet green pasture." She looked back at Papa for approval.

Papa grinned with pride, "I know just the place." With that, Papa, arms full of pots, walked around Chosen, through the court-yard to a small wooden fence at the other end. He beckoned Chosen to follow, and the two started down a small dirt trail, toting their pots.

For a while, only green fields surrounded Chosen. The horizon, flat and unchanging made her wonder how long they would be walking to find the mountaintop she had talked about. Her arms tired carrying the pots. Coming around a bend in the trail, Chosen noticed the trail dipping down a short hill. There at the bottom of the hill, in the middle of the greenery was a mud pit. The swampy mess of damp dirt and sludge looked ghastly and smelled even worse. She had inadvertently stopped walking at the sight of it.

"You'll need to come closer, Chosen," Papa signaled to her.

Chosen shook her head. Surely they had made a wrong turn. She stared at the site in confusion. It looked nothing like what she had trusted Papa for.

Papa placed His pots down next to the bog and came back to collect Chosen. "You look conflicted," He noted as He began to take pots out of Chosen's arms.

She nodded, "I was expecting something a little more, pretty."

Papa understood. He ushered her over to the bog and put down the rest of the pots, "Remarkable flowers, aren't they?"

"Yes, Papa, they are stunning. Where did they come from? I didn't see any like them in the courtyard."

"These are special. They need great care. I find it best to cultivate them in the throne room."

She mustered up a smile while holding her nose. Inwardly she wondered why this should be the best place to plant throne room flowers.

Papa picked up a fiery orange flower with long, curly petals, "Do you know what I have planted in this pot, Chosen?"

Chosen shook her head, grateful for some explanation.

"In these pots, I have planted greatness."

"Greatness?"

He nodded, "Greatness. It's beautiful. When it's planted,"

Papa paused and took out a small shovel from his back pocket, "watch what happens." Bending down right by the swamp, Papa found a fairly solid bit of mud in which to dig a hole. After digging, Papa removed the flower from the pot and placed it tenderly in the swamp, tucking it into the mud. He smiled, taking Chosen's hand, "Now we stand back and wait."

Chosen furrowed her brow in confusion, but held Papa's hand tightly as she began to feel the ground shake. She blinked, trying to make sense of what she was seeing. Far off in the horizon, a large mountain rose up from the previously flat landscape. After it had settled, Chosen saw water cascade from the sides of the mountain. Her eyes caught the sight of the edges of the bog, now drying up, turning green, and smelling sweet. Greatness had been planted, and everything had changed.

"That's incredible." Chosen whispered.

"So many think greatness is a thing to achieve, but greatness is not found in a destination or occupation. Greatness lies in my flowers blooming in the fields in which they are planted. It is not about achieving, it's about being." Papa looked at Chosen by His side, "Every child of mine is fitted with greatness. The power of greatness lies not in where it is established, but what it establishes.

A flower planted in a bog can still move a mountain. Do you see, Chosen?"

Clearly she could – she had. She planned to plant the flower in the beauty she could see. He had planted the flower in the beauty that could be. She looked up at Papa and decided that potential must be highly alluring to Him.

It had been an amazing sight, but Chosen still wondered what it all had to do with her.

"I have one more thing I must show you." Papa took Chosen's hand and led her away from the newly planted flower. They continued on down the trail leaving the flowerpots where they were. Through the trees and around another bend, Chosen's heart raced as they came across a new landscape. Only minutes before everything had looked so flat, but now she stood with Papa on a cliff's edge overlooking a large valley. Beyond them stood a wide and marvelous mountain range. Waterfalls streamed down the mountains into a blue lake at the bottom of the vibrant green valley.

"It's astonishing," she whispered as her eyes continued to discover the unique details of the land.

Papa squeezed her hand, "remember to breathe, Chosen."

"It's unbelievable, Papa."

"Chosen," He said, "it's here that I planted your greatness."

Chosen gently dropped Papa's hand and covered her mouth. Her eyes widened, "How? When?"

"It didn't take much," Papa said matter-of-factly, "Love does most of the work. You were faithful to be rooted and grounded in My love." He turned her towards Himself and collected her hands. "You have been blooming and growing for a while, developing deep roots. I wanted you to be aware of how you are transforming my Kingdom in doing so. As you take time to know My love and let it flow through your life, the landscape changes," He grinned now from ear to ear, "and I rather like what you've done with the place."

Chosen looked away bashfully as He squeezed her hands.

"The world may never know your name, Chosen, but that is of little consequence. For the Kingdom itself testifies to your life." Papa turned towards the mountains again, "And what a significant life it is."

Chosen nodded quietly, overwhelmed, but received His words.

"I just wanted you to know." Papa wrapped His arm around her shoulder as she leaned into Him. He kissed her head, "Chosen, would you like to take a walk through this lovely piece of land?"

He felt her take a deep breath, "Yes, Papa," she finally spoke, "Yes, I would."

He took her hand and led Chosen farther down the path towards the blue lake at the bottom of the valley. Admiring the fragrances and vantage points along the way, Chosen and Papa enjoyed each other's company while they hiked through the landscape birthed by the greatness of a loving child.

A FIELD OF DREAMS

I T SEEMED LIKE DUSK. Though Invested knew that in this
place, dusk was as obscure as dawn. There was no need to
awaken the day or the night in these parts, for time was quite
inconsequential. Because of this, Invested knew that there must
be a reason for the dimming of light.

The field he stood in was rather nondescript. All around
him, the grass stood tall, swaying across small hills. But as the light
continued to dim, the edges of the grass blades began to glow gold,
illuminating the field below his feet. Unsure if he had arrived at his

destination, he thought it best to double check his invitation.

Curiously, as he took it out from his pocket, he noticed lines upon it beginning to glow gold like the grass beneath him. As he watched, these lines on the invitation began to take shape, and soon there was a surprising addition – a map. The map on the invitation showed a path of varying colors swirling through the great field and leading to a flat area. Invested wondered what the colors might mean, and how to follow them seeing as how all of the grass was glowing gold. As Invested turned his attention back to the field, he noticed that a patch of grass in front of him was now glowing a red color. As soon as he stepped into the red grass, a new patch of grass before him began to glow purple, just as he saw it on the map. One step after another, Invested walked through the luminous field over hills and meadows and finally found himself at a flat clearing. He couldn't help but laugh.

"Is it shocking?" Papa joked from behind him.

"I should have guessed." Invested admitted.

Papa nodded. "Perhaps. You are quite the puzzle solver." Smiling, he approached Invested with open arms and embraced him.

"It's a nice field." Invested offered as he looked again at

the bases, foul lines, and pitcher's mound. The grass was intensely green, and the boundary lines were pristinely white. It was the most beautiful baseball field Invested had ever seen.

"I was hoping you'd like it," Papa replied, "How about we try her out?" Without waiting for a response, Papa tossed Invested a perfectly worn baseball glove, and the two headed out to the field.

"You pitch, Invested."

Invested began to walk towards the pitcher's mound, then turned to Papa, "What am I pitching?"

Papa smiled, and held up his hand, asking for a moment. He walked behind the backstop and picked up a canvas bag. He walked over to Invested, handed him the bag, and then resumed his position beside home plate. Invested continued on to the pitcher's mound where he dropped the bag and looked out over the field. Bending down, he opened the bag. He'd never seen anything like them. Inside the bag sat strange clear orbs, and inside each of them danced little flames of light. They were impressive under the dimming sky. Invested reached down to pick one up, finding the consistency of the ball to be flexible, yet delicate. He wondered if he might pop one by handling it too hard. He looked up at Papa, puzzled.

"I'm ready!" Papa said, swinging the bat.

Invested looked back down at the balls, shaking his head, "Papa," he paused trying to contemplate what to do, "I think I might break them - whatever they are."

"They're studier than they feel, Invested. Come on! I'm so ready!" Papa bent his knees to find his balance.

Invested was mesmerized by the strange spheres and took little notice of Papa, primed and ready to swing. Papa just watched him, and smiled. He finally dropped his bat and stood up straight.

"They're dreams!" Papa cried out.

"Dreams?" Invested rolled them around in his hands. "Fascinating." He studied them observing their colors and texture.

Papa loved Invested's inquisitive nature. "Invested?" Papa called again.

Invested finally looked back up at Papa.

"Those are your dreams, Invested," Papa said calmly and grinned, "why don't you pitch one to me?"

"Oh, right, Papa, right." It was time to get back in the game, and though he wasn't sure how this all worked, he reached down and picked up one of the dreams. It still felt fragile in his hand.

Papa took His stance, wiggled His hips, and pulled back the bat.

As Invested drew back his arm, he felt the dream firm up, as if preparing for a journey. Just before the ball left his hand, it felt solid and sure, like a baseball. Flying towards home plate, the dream began to glow brighter, and the moment Papa hit it, a fusion of light and sound burst from inside the dream, cascading all around it like a firework. The dream soared above Invested's head, beyond second base, to the outskirts of the field. And just when you thought it might land, that little dream swooped straight up into the sky again and began to gallivant in all directions over the field, flying up and down and circling around. It was quite content to remain in flight.

"They like to fly," Papa explained.

Invested watched the dream hurling back and forth and around the field, in all its fantastic light and color. It was beautiful.

"Pitch me another, Invested!" Papa finally shouted.

With the first dream flying happily overhead, Invested pitched another. In a short time there were nearly twenty dreams flying above, like an amusing light show. Invested reached down into the bag and pulled out a large dream, one his hands could barely grip. He wondered how he was going to throw this one to Papa.

"It's okay," Papa affirmed, "I'm fond of the big ones, just pitch it!"

Trying not to think too much about the physics of the problem, Invested drew back his arm balancing the large dream. With a deep breath, he slung it right over home plate.

The dream hit the bat and rose straight up to join the flock of other dreams, now swarming above. The sky was full of great and colorful balls of light. It was stunning, like a promenading starry night. At times the dreams would fly in formation only to burst forth into solo acrobatic routines.

Invested stood back from the pitcher's mound looking up at the sky. Papa dropped the bat and walked towards Invested.

"Beautiful, isn't it? Your dreams are beautiful." Papa mused.

"They look better in the sky." Invested remarked.

"It's a team effort." Papa placed his hand on Invested's shoulder.

"There are so many."

Papa smirked and patted Invested on the back, "and this is such a small sampling of your dreams, Invested."

Papa watched Invested try and follow the dreams as they danced about the sky. Moments later, Invested felt something touch his hands. Papa was handing him a large net, like one used to catch butterflies, though it was a great deal bigger. As Invested took the net, he thought he knew what the net must be for, but he gave Papa a questioning look.

Papa raised an eyebrow. His eyes twinkled with a hint of adventure. "Now, it's time to catch one." Invested looked back up into the sky and over at Papa again.

"Papa, how do you expect me to catch one of those?

"That's what the net is for." Papa replied nonchalantly.

Invested looked at the net and back at Papa, and shook his head, "Have you been watching those little guys dashing around up there? Sometimes they're so fast, I can't even see them!"

Papa simply nodded his head in encouragement, "It's best to wait for them to fly close to the ground."

Invested meandered out towards the outfield a bit, net in hand.

"Invested, keep your eye on the ball." Papa cheered.

Invested tried to keep his eyes focused on the dreams above as they swooshed and swirled. Occasionally they would descend down, at a lightening speed, and swoop past Invested. He could feel the wind pass him as they did. Papa's voice rose again.

"Choose one, Invested, and stare it down! Don't take your eyes off of it!"

He looked overhead to see the great speedway of dreams and tried decisively to find one he could keep his eye on. With great concentration his eyes followed a smallish dream with blue flames burning inside. It flew furiously, up and down, rounding to the left and turning abruptly to the right. The more he watched it, the more it seemed to slow down, until finally the little dream stopped altogether, and began heading straight towards Invested.

"Hold your net out, Invested!" Papa cried.

Invested kept his eyes peeled on the dream as it approached him, and lifted the net overhead. Soon, the dream gently found its way right into the net, where it settled as if it wanted a nap. Invested looked back at Papa with surprise

"Great job, Invested. Executed like a pro," Papa nodded with pride.

Invested walked to Papa with a dream tucked safety in his net. He held out his catch, unsure what to do next.

Papa looked the dream over, "Oh, it's a good one."

Invested smiled.

Looking Invested straight in the eye, he instructed, "Now, you eat it."

"I what?" Invested wasn't sure if he'd heard Papa correctly.

"You eat it, and honestly the quicker the better, before it sneaks off again."

Invested wrinkled his brow as he slowly placed his hand inside the net to grab the dream. Once he had it balanced in his hand, he dropped the net and held the dream with both hands. It felt different. It wasn't like the jelly-ball it had been in the bag or the baseball it had been in his pitching hand. It felt soft, like a peach, and tingled with life. Invested looked up at Papa.

Papa shrugged his shoulders, "I have that effect."

Invested drew the dream towards his nose and sniffed. It smelled sweet and expectant, if something could smell expectant. He sighed and at last took a bite.

He could feel the life that tingled within the dream flow down his throat and finally reside in his belly. It was a strange sensation, to eat a dream, to feel it begin to stir life within you. It was as if the dream itself was hosting a rally within to win the allegiance of his spirit, mind, soul, and body. Things were happening inside him, and all he could have explained was that he felt more alive now than before he took the bite.

Papa loved moments like these, to see the ones He loved enjoying the wonders of the Kingdom.

"Am I to eat it all, Papa?" Invested looked at Papa wondering if the lesson had come to an end.

Papa smiled and looked at the dream before Invested and then up into the sky full of dancing dreams, "Eat as much as you like. Eat much or eat little. All I ask is that you would enjoy the feast."

Invested took account of his settings. What a marvelous and odd thing to be before Papa eating a dream, under a sky illuminated by dreams.

"You wonder what it all means, don't you?" Papa asked.

Invested nodded, dream still in hand, now beginning to drip an iridescent juice down his fingers.

"But the truth is," Papa said smirking, "you are too observant and clever for me to simply explain this mystery, so I offer you the floor. Tell me what you have seen."

And although it would have been easy for Papa to unravel the tale, Invested admitted he desired a go at it. His eyes searched the landscape as he searched his mind for clues. Soon something began to stand out to Invested as significant.

"The dreams," Invested began, "all came from you. You handed me the bag full of dreams."

Papa grinned. "The capacity to dream, the tendency to dream, the propensity to dream for certain things, true. I gave that to you. But the bag was filled with your own dreams, things birthed in your own heart, in your own mind. I just have a habit of hanging on to them all."

Invested nodded with understanding. "I had a bag full of dreams, they all had potential, all teemed with light. But something changed when I pitched them to you."

"There is something remarkable that happens when you pick up a dream, turn your eyes towards Me, and then offer Me the dream. Did you notice how the dream changed, Invested?"

"It firmed up. It began to take shape." Invested answered.

"Even the loftiest dreams, sense possibility when directed at Me. For with Me all things are possible. Dreams know this. When you begin to pitch, they begin to prepare themselves to transfer from the realm of imagination to reality."

Invested peered overhead to watch the dreams again flying above. He nodded his head towards the sky, "Those then, those are dreams that have become possible, is that right?"

"More than possible. Alive. Fused with purpose, power, and longevity, released to dazzle all who would cast their eyes on them.

A dream touched by my hand, becomes a vessel for my kingdom to expand. They take flight because they are so full of life. And there they wait," Papa directed his vision towards the sky, "in this field of dreams, for one who might see them, one who might catch them, one who might eat them and let them to come to fruition. For that Invested, is their greatest desire."

Papa closed his eyes, "I wish you could see it, Invested. I wish you could see the sight of the field full of all of the dreams of man. No dream is ever lost, you see. When they come to me, they reside together up there, and so they have since man first dreamed. How remarkable the sight when one comes and catches an ancient dream, which like fine wine has been twirling and swirling throughout the ages with ever increasing expectancy. For to dream is to invest, not only that you might carry a dream, but that others might carry one of yours in a day or a year a generation or so. I've even seen dreams merge and multiply up there. It's simply incredible."

Invested stood still as Papa grew silent. He looked up into the sky as his ears tuned in to the sound of the flying dreams – this majestic wind. Papa watched him joyously. He quietly approached and gently placed his hand on Invested. The wind around them increased as Papa, for a moment, unveiled the sound of the dreams of all men from all time to the ears of this beloved son. And in that incredible moment Invested could hear the sound of a kingdom – of voices, and songs, and movement and abundant life dictated solely by the wind above. About the time that Invested thought the sound might crush him, Papa removed his hand and took a step back.

"You have invested in my kingdom," Papa spoke at last. "Your dreams are good, and not one has been lost. You have a good arm and pitch well. I wanted to invite you again, Invested, to throw me a new dream or find a dream you might like to taste, to set your eyes on it, and catch it. Whatever delights you. There is no failure here. For the dreams of man cannot shift my goodness or my love. I am faithful to complete the good work I started in you and in this world. So when I invite you to dream, I invite you to play. Do you see? It is not a test. It's an invitation, simply to do something with me."

Invested stood drinking in fresh freedom.

Papa took a deep breath. He picked up Invested's baseball glove that was resting on the ground beside them. "Play with me?" He asked as He offered Invested the glove again.

Invested was standing with his hands on his hips gazing again up into the bountiful sky of dreams. He looked down at the glove before him, and up at Papa.

"I'd like that," He said simply reaching for the glove. By the time Invested hit the pitcher's mound again, the canvas bag that had previously been emptied of dreams, was full again.

Throughout the kingdom the crack of the bat and the whirl of dreams could be heard as Invested pitched and Papa launched dream upon dream high above the field into the realms of possibility and hope and life.

LEGACY

DESTINED STOOD SILENTLY IN THE GREAT HALL. He fingered his baseball hat and pulled it off. Rolling it in his back pocket, he reached into his other pocket and pulled out the invitation.

He read it carefully again looking around the spacious room.

This must be it. Destined shrugged his shoulders. Cream walls stood mightily around him, trimmed with intricate silver patterns. The room had no windows, and yet boasted refreshing light. Curious, he thought, that Papa had left all that blank space on the walls. But knowing Papa, he knew the room was purposefully constructed.

Although he could have whiled away the time admiring the silver trim, Destined instead sat down on the floor and pulled a pouch of jacks from his pocket. The floor resounded as Destined bounced the ball.

Bounce. Scoop. Bounce. Scoop. Bounce.

"Scoop," said Papa, grabbing up the jacks.

"When did you get here, Papa?"

"Sneaky, aren't I?" Papa playfully patted Destined's arm.

"Yes, Papa. And I'll have you know I was doing really well in that round of jacks before you showed up and stole my turn!"

Papa chuckled and the two playfully batted each other.

"I'm glad you came, Destined. It's always good to spend time with you." Papa lovingly stroked the boy's head. "Now, let's see." Papa stood to his feet and turned around in a circle, studying the large blank walls.

"Did you forget to hang some pictures or something, Papa?" Destined kidded as he watched Papa mosey around the room. He was thinking about something, though Destined hadn't the foggiest idea what.

"No," Papa smiled, as he continued to walk around the room, "This room is quite perfect." Papa finally paused, staring up at one of the walls. "I have wanted to show you this room for a long time, Destined. I want you to see something very special." Papa walked to the wall in front of Destined and placed his hands on it. Something was happening. Electricity, or something like it, was being released from Papa to the wall. Papa just stood there, hands outstretched.

At first, Destined could not see any purpose to this little game. But something caught his eye. Destined began to see words appear at the very top of the wall. Names. And more names. Names began to fade in, as if an invisible artist was now painting on the giant blank canvas. As more and more names began to appear, Destined could see it was a chart of sorts. Names were spreading all around the room, creating a waterfall as they cascaded down the walls. The names multiplied and lines joined them. And then he saw it. *Destined.* His own name. His name had appeared in the vast family tree now adorning the walls.

"My family tree?" Destined looked at Papa.
Papa nodded and smiled, teary-eyed. Papa placed His hands on the wall again and slowly leaned in until His forehead kissed the family tree, "So beautiful."

Destined approached the wall, drawing near to his name. He saw the familiar names of those who came before and the unfamiliar names of those who came after. He looked above and all around the room, overwhelmed with the sight of so many names. So many lives led to his own. He had so many questions about those who had come before, and those who would come after. The magnitude of life and the abundance of family left him simply offering Papa a bewildered look.

Papa nodded knowingly, and then directed His eyes towards Destined's name on the wall. Destined's eyes followed as he noticed a glimmer of blue light begin to emerge from around his name. Destined looked up at Papa, waiting for an explanation. But Papa gave none. Instead He just nodded again, eyes directed at the name. Destined felt a great urge to lift his hand and touch his name on the wall. He looked back at Papa requesting permission. Papa smiled with assurance. Destined, turning back to his name, let his fingers fall softly upon it.

The moment of contact released an electric-like surge through Destined's arm, though it didn't hurt. He could only describe the feeling as love. This love raced through every fiber of his body. As this love covered his ears, he began to hear something wonderful. In a room that was quiet just moments before, Destined could hear the sound of a dear hymn, rising in a chorus of voices with a full orchestra. The acoustics made Destined wonder if he had actually been relocated to a concert hall, though his eyes confirmed he hadn't gone anywhere. The music was so surprising at first, Destined let go of the wall. At once the music stopped, only to begin again when Destined returned his fingers:

Then sings my soul, my Savior God to Thee

How great Thou art, how great Thou art.

Destined closed his eyes drinking in the song. As the last chorus rang out in his ears, he caught his breath. He had not realized he was holding it. His fingers then slipped and landed on a nearby name, startling Destined, as love again surged through his arm and another song overtook him. He had not heard this song before. A myriad of instruments and melodies rang out, different from his own song, but just as breathtaking. Eyeing his own name again, Destined had an idea. With one hand touching the new name, he placed his other hand back on his own name, and then it came. Love surged through both arms and two songs interlaced in perfect harmony resounded through his ears. Destined's arms began to tremble and his eyes began to water. The beauty of the love and the music was beyond reason. When he could not take any more, his hands dropped, and he fell to his knees.

Papa walked to him and knelt down beside him, wrapping his arm around Destined and drawing him close.

"Your life has a beautiful song, Destined. I love to listen to it." Papa spoke softly over his little head, "Now, hold tight to me, Destined. Our day wouldn't be complete unless I show you what I'm about to." With that, Papa looked up at the walls and at once every name began to glow. He held Destined tight under his arm and raised the other hand to touch the wall.

Destined imagined that the surge of love itself should have ended his life, so great was its magnitude. But under Papa's wing, he was able to endure it. The powerful sound of all the songs from all the ages, from every person that had preceded and would follow Destined was tangible. He thought for a moment the music might stand up and ask him to dance around the room. He gripped Papa with all he had until finally Papa let go of the wall. Though the walls had been blank, the masterpiece was now clear. This family was designed with wonder.

The room was silent again, and still. Papa loosened his embrace around Destined. "Powerful."

Destined nodded. Papa appeared mesmerized, staring at the names.

"You see the names. You hear the music, Destined. But there is more." Papa took Destined's hand and backed up to the middle of the room so both could have a good view. Suddenly a name near the top of the wall began to glow again. Destined instinctively clung close to Papa. Papa stroked his head as if to reassure him, this time he wouldn't be so affected by what was about to happen. Destined could hear a voice, a voice that came from the glowing name. He could understand the words. It was the sound of that person praying. As the prayer ended a glowing orb formed out of the glowing name and floated to another name on the family tree. Then, a few more names began to glow. Destined heard more prayers and the orbs flew through the room like shooting stars. Soon the room was a hub of activity. A multitude of prayers echoed through the room while glowing orbs soared from one name to another, from one side of the room to the other, wall to wall, high to low and back again.

"I hear their prayers, Destined, you see? But sometimes the answer comes to another in the family. Look." Papa pointed down to Destined's name. Destined saw a barrage of glowing orbs hit his name coming from every which way around the room. Likewise, orbs repeatedly formed from his name and traversed around the room.

"It's a fireworks show, Papa."

Papa smiled, "My favorite kind. I hear them all, Destined, every prayer. And I am not slow to answer as some consider slow. Rather, I am strategic, working on a canvas that expands through time. My son, your prayers have been greatly effective. You have put on quite a show there." Papa patted Destined's shoulder. Destined marveled at the sight of prayers being lifted up and answered throughout the generations.

Papa knelt down beside Destined and whispered in his ear, "Look, my child, beyond the names." Destined at first wasn't sure what Papa meant, but as he gazed as best he could beyond the names, the names themselves began to blur and the walls became like a soft veil. All he could see for miles and miles beyond the curtain was a beautiful scene of hills and mountains and a Kingdom nestled within them, abounding with life.

"It's what I'm building," Papa whispered, "through these people whose names you see." Papa looked back at Destined to make sure he understood, "I have drawn up my plans since before the beginning of time and I have hidden pieces of them here and there, throughout the hearts of men, throughout the ages. We were all meant to be together. This was always My hope."

Papa took Destined's small hand and walked towards the veil to get a closer look. "You and your family, Destined are co-laborers with me for this Kingdom, and someday it will be on earth as it is in heaven. This is the fulfillment of the promise that the dwelling place of Papa would be with man. All you have said, and done, and prayed, I have used for this purpose. Clever, aren't I?"

Destined stood silently for a moment, then looked up with a sly grin, "Yes, Papa, very clever." They exchanged smiles and a lighthearted laugh.

"Each of you are building a legacy, passing down tools of the trade, that the Kingdom would expand. And we are getting closer, Destined. I long for this restoration."

"Me too," Destined finally said trying to take it all in.

"Thank you for loving Me, Destined. Thank you for trusting Me." Papa turned to Destined and hugged Him.

Destined embraced Papa. His mind filled with the thoughts of legacy and purpose interwoven through the ages, finally trickling down to him. What a joy to partner with Papa, what a privilege to be His own. Destined could have easily stayed right there clinging to

Papa forever. Instead, he heard His playful, familiar voice.

"How about a rematch?"

Destined looked up at Papa, "Of course," Destined agreed, "but no cheating."

"I never cheat, little one," Papa said with passion, "but I do tend to win." He winked at Destined and walked back to the middle of the room.

Destined pulled out his pouch of jacks and the two sat down in the middle of the great hall bouncing and scooping and laughing and jesting, filling the land with sounds of joy, while the Kingdom continued to expand just beyond the veil.

FOR MY SCRIBE

P APA WHISPERED AS HE LEANED FORWARD in his wingback chair, "You look sleepy, Scribe." He grinned.

Scribe rubbed her eyes and stretched her hand which lovingly held a calligraphy pen.

"Perhaps we should take a little break from writing these invitations?"

"I'll be okay, Papa. I just need to readjust." Scribe reached her arms up in the air to release the tension that had built up in her back from leaning over the large wooden desk in her library.

"I have something for you, Scribe," Papa said, "I wanted to wait for the perfect moment, and I believe this is it." Papa reached over to a nearby shelf covered with large hardback books and pulled an envelope from between two of them. He smiled gently as he held it securely in both of his hands. He looked down at the old, worn envelope. Scribe sat, quietly watching his every move. The moment felt significant. She sensed Papa had waited a very long time for it. She wondered if it was appropriate to move, or even to breathe. Slowly leaning forward, she placed her pen on the desk.

Papa's eyes welled with tears. "These invitations have been very precious to me, Scribe, and you have done well to transcribe my heart. But there is one you have yet to open and explore." With those simple words he placed the worn envelope before her on the desk.

There was no pomp or circumstance to the envelope. No intricate filigree. No graphic delights. No colors really. In fact, if anything, it merely looked old, yellowed with age. But the inscription was unmistakable. In the middle of the envelope, written with a calligraphy pen much like the one she just placed on the table, were the words, For my Scribe.

"It's for me?" Scribe delighted. "It's my invitation?" She

stared intently at the envelope as her eyes filled with tears. She knew instinctively Papa would not let her tears fall, but she hoped He might permit them this time.

Papa knelt down beside her chair. He looked on her with a freeing love. Nodding, He allowed her tears. "You are my patient child. I know how you wait. I know how you wonder." He tenderly rubbed her shoulders with the affections of a father, "But please know," He whispered, "You have not been forgotten. I have not looked past you or over you. I know this was unexpected. It was never your intent to receive, but it has always been my intention to give. I know you, Scribe. I know every part of you. You are my cherished child, and my dear friend. Truthfully, I am most thankful you agreed to be my scribe so that we might simply spend time together."

Scribe listened carefully to each word spilling from Papa's mouth, but became lost in her puddle of tears. She had never thought when she agreed to be His scribe for this assignment that His greatest intent would simply be, to spend time with her. She always believed her greatest priority was to listen carefully and write accurately, blessing His children, that they would know His love and His goodness towards them. Now she too held something that had become so precious in this journey, an invitation from His hand. Her fingers traced its edges and her eyes revered the dirt and fingerprints here and there. "You didn't write this just now, Papa. You have kept this for a long time, haven't you?"

He nodded with quiet tears falling down His cheeks. "I wrote this," he drew a slow breath, "when I first thought of you." He smiled through His tears, "It has actually kept quite well."

His first thought of her - the thought was thankfully beyond Scribe's understanding. For if she had fully understood the implications of her invitation being penned before there was time or light or land or men, she might have fainted with the weight of this revelation of His love. Instead, she simply turned to Him and placed one hand on His cheek saying, "My patient, Papa. How long you have waited."

"Let us dry our tears, dear Scribe. It is time to open the envelope." As Papa brushed away Scribe's tears, Scribe brushed away Papa's and they grinned. Scribe took one more look at the little worn envelope and opened it.

Her nose wrinkled as she grinned from ear to ear, and slightly rolled her eyes. She looked over to Papa who resumed his position in the wingback chair opposite the desk. "What's so funny?" Papa smirked, knowing full well the irony of the contents of the invitation.

"It says," Scribe tried to contain herself, "Meet me in the library."

Papa clapped His hands, "I've always thought you so obedient, and in this case, extremely prompt."

Scribe shook her head as she looked at the invitation again making sure she didn't miss something. Looking up at Papa, she lifted her arms up and sighed, "Well. Here I am, Papa!" It mattered little to Scribe that she was already exactly where the invitation required her to be. For she knew from experience that what came after the invitation was always thrilling and she was ripe with expectation of adventure. "What are we going to do?"

"We're going to wait." Papa said calmly.

"Wait?" Scribe was confused.

"Yes, wait," Papa said confidently, "For another. He should be here any moment."

"Another?" Scribe looked around her little library trying to consider who he might be. She hadn't a clue, which pleased Papa to no end, for He loved surprises.

Scribe leaned back in the chair. She looked around the room, biding her time, expecting a knock at the door. But there was nothing. Just Papa, patiently waiting in His chair, resting and enjoying the breeze from the large balcony behind Him. Scribe rose from her chair and walked around the room, stopping to admire the treasures on the bookshelves. Her hands patted Papa's recipe book of pies. He had even illustrated it, the pictures revealing His humorous side – a series of drawings of Papa holding up pies and grinning. On the shelf below was a jewelry box, which held a necklace whose round charm had a wing etched on one side and a fin on the other. She came across another shelf that held a worn baseball glove and a bag of jacks. Beside them sat a small music box. Scribe opened it affectionately.

As she recalled His beloved adventures, she suddenly felt heat on her back, through her arms, and in her wrists. She quickly turned to Papa in want of an explanation. Papa nodded, "I think He's here."

Turning to Papa, the heat began to leave Scribe's body from the palms of her hand. She stared at her hands wondering what was happening, "Who's here? What's going on?"

"Scribe, how does your back feel, now," Papa asked, "and your wrists?"

Scribe took a moment to twirl her hands around and stretch

out her back. She smiled. Everything that had been tired and sore moments prior, was refreshed and pain free. "I feel great. I feel like I could write hundreds of invitations now!"

"Really?" Papa said, "I think He'll be happy to hear that."

"Who?"

"Me." said a voice from somewhere inside Scribe. She looked around the room. Did she hear that out loud? Was it in her mind?

It spoke again, "Don't be afraid. It's Me."

Scribe approached Papa, "Did you hear that?"

Papa nodded, "Scribe, He is an old friend. More than a friend."

She shook her head trying to understand.

"Holy Spirit has come, Scribe."

"Holy Spirit?"

"Yes. And now I will leave you two to get to work, or play, as the case may be." Papa rose from His chair and walked to the door of the library. Scribe dashed after Him.

"Papa, where are You going – what about the invitation, my invitation? Aren't we going on a great journey?"

Papa stood before her. He placed His hands on her shoulders. "Yes, we are. A great journey, Scribe. A new journey."

Her wide eyes begged Him to stay.

"There is a part of my love that only He can show you, a part of my plan that only He can accomplish, a type of adventure that only He can lead you on. Believe me. It is better that I go. But I will return, Scribe. This story is just beginning."

Her hands wiped her wet cheeks, missing Him already.

He turned to open the door and Scribe felt His embrace, though clearly His hands were at His sides.

Papa turned, smiling, "He's a good comforter." And with that Papa left the library.

Scribe took a deep breath. She looked around the empty room. *What should I say to Holy Spirit? Where was He anyway?*

"Here," came a still quiet voice within, "I'm here."

"Holy Spirit?" Scribe asked tentatively, "This is strange for me."

"I understand," He replied.

"How do I talk to someone I can't see?"

"Faithfully." He offered, quietly.

She walked back over to the desk and sat down.

"Scribe, you have invited many to spend time with Papa. I was curious if you might do the same for Me?"

"Write invitations for You?" She fiddled with her pen.

"Yes."

As Scribe recalled the first time Papa had asked her to write an invitation for Him, feelings of excitement and joy rose within. Writing the invitations had opened a door to knowing Him and His love so deeply, how could she pass up another opportunity? She had no idea what this would look like, to write invitations for One you couldn't see, but the unknown suddenly appealed to her.

Scribe nodded, "I will do it." Smiling, she opened the desk drawer to grab some paper. She laughed as waves of joy rolled from her head to her toes. She trusted in the reality of His unseen presence, and felt the comfort and familiarity of a dear friend. She readied herself for round two of the invitations.

"You won't need those." Holy Spirit said as Scribe straightened her paper and prepared her fountain pen.

Leaning back in her chair, Scribe looked up at the balcony. He was right, she wouldn't need her pen, or her paper. She left them on the table, stood up and walked out onto the balcony. She was beginning to understand these new invitations would be different. From somewhere deep within her a melody began to rise. She sang to the great landscape beyond the balcony a song she'd never heard with words she barely knew – a song He was singing within her. And somewhere beyond the Kingdom, the Holy Spirit released a new invitation to one who was patiently waiting to hear His voice.

ABOUT THE AUTHOR

SARA RUST grew up overseas and returned to the United States to complete a film degree at Northwestern University. Following graduation, she moved to southern Illinois where she was involved in community development as a missionary. In 2009, Sara moved to Redding, California to complete a Master's in Education and spend time teaching scores of action-packed third and fourth graders. Storytelling has weaved its way though every chapter, and has now, after much patience, won a more prominent place in her life.

Sara is an innovative storyteller of page, stage, and screen, journeying through life catching stories where they fly. Equipped with an overactive imagination, she loves writing stories that tell of the great Love that pursues us all.

Follow her journey at saramrust.com.

BASILEIA

"The land behind the silver door exploded with light and color. No one knew how big Basileia was or how many lifetimes it would take to find out. It was here the children would while away their days, free to do what they truly loved."

Basileia (Greek for *kingdom*) is the whimsical story of a village whose children spend their days in a hidden land. But when the children mysteriously begin to forget about the land behind the silver door, one brave girl must find a way to remember before Basileia is lost forever. Let wonder and dreams be awakened again as you too journey behind the silver door and discover what brings you life. Delight your heart with this timeless and inspiring storybook for young and old.

AVAILABLE ON AMAZON

KINGDOM TOOLS FOR TEACHING

"If you've been looking for how to create a godly revolution around you in the classroom, then you've found what you've been looking for. This book isn't a way to subversively have devotions or church in the classroom. In these pages you will find a template to show students freedom, love, joy, righteousness, hope and power."

Danny Silk, best-selling author of ***Keep Your Love On*** and ***Culture of Honor***

Kingdom Tools for Teaching brings both inspiration and practical tools to empower and activate you in bringing the Kingdom of God to ANY classroom. This is not a manual. This is the testimony of our breakthroughs and the tools that came from them. It is our heart to share these tools to inspire you to find your own and to adapt ours for your own classroom and school. We invite you to join us on a journey of stepping out of the mundane and into an adventure with Him that will shape students lives, the course of education and maybe even history itself.

Made in the USA
Middletown, DE
22 March 2022

62995310R00089